Contents

1 Articles: *the* before general concepts   5
2 Articles: *a/an* before noun phrases   6
3 When do I use capital letters?   7

Test 1   8

4 When do I use *when*, *if* and *whether*?   10
5 Punctuation: commas with discourse markers   11
6 Punctuation: using apostrophes   12

Test 2   13

7 Common spelling mistakes   15
8 Spelling: one word or two?   16
9 Adjective forms   17

Test 3   18

10 Using prepositions: with nouns   20
11 Using prepositions: after verbs   21
12 Using prepositions: describing trends and changes   22

Test 4   23

13 Describing statistics: using prepositions   25
14 Describing statistics: nouns   26
15 Describing statistics: verbs   27

Test 5   28

16 *Number* and *amount*   30
17 Making comparisons   31
18 Expressing contrast   32

Test 6   33

19 Countable and uncountable nouns   35
20 Singular and plural verb forms   36
21 *It, they* and *them*   37

Test 7   38

22 Verbs: *being* and *having*   40
23 Commonly confused verbs: *join/attend, give/provide*   41
24 Verb collocations   42

Test 8   43

25 Commonly confused nouns: *habits, customs* and *practices*   45
26 Commonly confused nouns: *effect, influence* and *impact*   46
27 Commonly confused nouns: time words   47

Test 9   48

28 Using nouns: *appearance* and *communication*   50
29 Using nouns and adjectives: *male* or *men*?   51
30 Using nouns and adjectives: *Britain, British* or *Briton*?   52

Test 10   53

Answer key   55

●●● Julie Moore

Common mistakes at

IELTS Advanced

... and how to avoid them

CAMBRIDGE
UNIVERSITY PRESS

CAMBRIDGE UNIVERSITY PRESS
Cambridge, New York, Melbourne, Madrid, Cape Town, Singapore, São Paulo, Delhi

Cambridge University Press
The Edinburgh Building, Cambridge CB2 8RU, UK

www.cambridge.org
Information on this title: www.cambridge.org/9780521692472

First published 2007
Reprinted 2007

Printed in the United Kingdom at the University Press, Cambridge

A catalogue record for this publication is available from the British Library

ISBN 978-0-521-69247-2 paperback

Produced by Kamae Design, Oxford

1 Articles: *the* before general concepts

1 Tick the correct sentence in each pair.

1 a Many people are worried about the bad effects of mobiles on brain.
  b Many people are worried about the bad effects of mobiles on the brain.
2 a We need to look at factors such as the availability of health care.
  b We need to look at factors such as availability of health care.

We use *the* before nouns which describe a general type of thing rather than a specific example of that thing:

These are problems for students living away from **the family**.
We don't know the effects of such chemicals on **the body**.
The role of **the student** *at university level varies greatly from country to country.*
Most of our business is carried out over **the telephone**.

The is also used before abstract nouns which describe a situation, a quality, a process or a change. These words are often followed by *of something*:

There is a problem with **the availability of** *clean water in some villages.*
The distribution of *income is uneven in most countries.*
On the whole, **the standard of** *living is better in urban areas.*
Many residents complained about **the frequency of** *bus services.*
This advance was brought about by **the development of** *antibiotics.*
He made a number of recommendations for **the improvement of** *staff training.*
☆ We use *the development/improvement, etc. of something* to describe a general process of change, but *developments/improvements, etc. in something* to describe specific changes:
We try to keep up-to-date with new **developments in** *information technology.*

2 Correct the mistake below.

> Doctors always stress importance of a balanced diet.

Doctors always stress ....

3 Are these sentences right or wrong? Correct those containing mistakes.

1 A diet high in cholesterol is bad for heart.
2 The introduction of computerised systems led to an increase in unemployment.
3 We all benefit from development of new technologies.
4 We were unhappy about quality of the food available.
5 Last year the airline saw a 20% improvement in delays.
6 There have been changes in the relationship between the teacher and the student.
7 Rates vary depending on standard of accommodation you choose.
8 She focused on the role of a family in a child's education.

Articles: *a/an* before noun phrases

1 Tick the correct sentence in each pair.

1 a The company has captured a significant share of the market.
  b The company has captured significant share of the market.
2 a I think they are also right to certain extent.
  b I think they are also right to a certain extent.

Don't forget to include *a/an* before an adjective + singular noun combination:
*He clearly has **a good understanding** of the issues.*
*Many students have **a part-time job** while studying.*

Notice the position of adverbs (*very, really, quite*, etc.) in these phrases:
*We have **a very high percentage** of women working in senior government posts.*
*There was **a really good atmosphere**.*
*In my view, this is **quite a strong argument**.*

Some common noun phrases to be careful with:
- *to a certain extent/degree: I agree with you **to a certain degree**.*
- *a wide range/variety: We have **a wide range of** books to choose from.*
- *a(n) large/small/equal number/amount: **an equal number of** men and women*
- *a high/large/small/greater proportion/percentage: **a small proportion of** patients*
- *a long time: I haven't seen her for **a long time**.*

2 Correct the mistake below.

All competitors should have equal chance of winning.

All competitors should ....

3 Use the words below in the same order to form correct sentences, adding any necessary articles or prepositions.

1 Only / small / number / troublemakers / were / responsible for / problems.
2 Computers / play / very / important / role / education / nowadays.
3 She / can't / afford to / study / full-time / basis.
4 Teenagers / should be / allowed / greater / degree / freedom.
5 They / have / slightly / different / approach to / studying.
6 We / had / one-week / intensive / training / course.
7 There / has been / gradual / increase / number / thefts.
8 They / offer / quite / wide / variety / courses.

When do I use capital letters?

1 Tick the correct sentence in each pair.

1 a She explained that Thai food often requires a lot of ingredients.
  b She explained that thai food often requires a lot of ingredients.
2 a Sixty percent of students enrolled at the university are male.
  b Sixty percent of students enrolled at the University are male.

Capital letters are always used for nouns in the following groups:

- countries: *Germany, the United States, Britain, the Czech Republic*, etc.
- towns, cities, states and regions: *Tokyo, Paris, Texas, New South Wales*, etc.
- nationalities, ethnic groups and religions – referring to people, languages or things from a country, region or culture:

  *Can you speak **Chinese**?* *You can hear he's **South African** from his accent.*
  *a **Buddhist** temple* *I'd like to learn more about **Asian** culture.*

- months and days of the week: *October, 9th April, Tuesday, Sunday*, etc.
  ☆ Capital letters are not used for the seasons: *spring, summer, autumn, winter*
- names of organisations and institutions: *the United Nations, the National Museum*
  Where a word like *museum, university, station* or *hospital* is part of the name of an institution, it has a capital letter: *Harvard University, Karachi Station, Rome Airport*
  However, when these words are not part of a name, they do not have a capital letter:
  *They built a new 100-bed **hospital** in the provincial capital.*
  *He first joined the **company** in 2003.*

☆ Also remember: *the Earth* (but not ~~the World~~), *the Third World/a Third World country, AIDS, CD/DVD* (plural *CDs/DVDs*).

2 Correct the mistake below.

I'm arriving at Heathrow airport on 12th January at 5.30 in the morning.

I'm arriving at ....

3 Add the correct punctuation, including capital letters, in the sentences below.

1 visitors to china should remember not to give a clock as a present
2 these customs are common in muslim countries such as saudi arabia
3 she started work for microsoft in july 2005
4 i went to university in geneva in switzerland
5 we took a taxi from york station to the royal york hotel in the city centre
6 this is a photo of me on wall street when we visited new york last summer
7 the red cross works throughout the world not just in third world countries
8 she hopes to compete for france in the european championships in august

TEST 1

1 Underline the correct article: *a/an, the* or – (no article).

1 This test measures *a/the/–* concentration of acid in *a/the/–* stomach.
2 It took *an/the/–* incredibly long time for the results to be announced.
3 There have been *an/the/–* improvements in *a/the/–* quality as well as *an/the/–* efficiency.
4 *A/The/–* high percentage of businesses fail in the first year.
5 The study found that *a/the/–* significant number of homes had two cars.
6 This shows *a/the/–* sharp decline in *a/the/–* proportion of aid allocated to health.
7 He studied the role of *an/the/–* extended family in caring for older people.
8 These reforms have succeeded to *a/the/–* certain extent.
9 All children should receive *a/the/–* basic education.
10 The HR department deals with *a/the/–* recruitment of new staff.
11 What is *a/the/–* significance of these figures?
12 She has *an/the/–* excellent communication skills.

2 The text below contains a number of mistakes with articles (*the, a/an*) and capital letters. Find the mistakes and correct them.

UNHCR
The UN Refugee Agency

The UN High Commissioner for Refugees (UNHCR) was established on 14 december, 1950. It was set up to protect refugees throughout World and to help in resolution of refugee problems. It has its headquarters in geneva, switzerland, but the Organisation has a staff of around 6,540 in 116 countries. Its main aim is to safeguard rights and well-being of refugees. Large proportion of the 20.8 million people which UNHCR helps are in third world, especially in countries in africa and asia. More than a quarter of the world's refugees, however, are in europe and united states, many of them seeking asylum.

3 Put the words below together to make three complete texts, adding any punctuation and extra words (such as articles or prepositions) necessary.

1 odile is french she was born lyon 21 september 1968 she moved britain 20 years ago and now has british citizenship she speaks english fluently but she still has quite strong french accent

2 corinne lives with her husband steve near melbourne australia steve is australian but corinne has german mother and american father she was born united states and met steve while they were both working europe

3 andré is travel photographer he lives switzerland but he spends large part of the year travelling around world last summer he went on long trip south america to photograph ancient inca temples

4 Rewrite the sentences below using the word given and making any changes necessary to keep the meaning the same.

1 The council wants to encourage new businesses to develop.
   development ....

2 His main role is to assess how good the service is for customers.
   quality ....

3 There has been an increase in the amount of goods transported by road.
   transportation ....

4 Whether mothers return to work often depends on whether childcare is available.
   availability ....

5 Many of the changes are due to the fact that tourism has grown in the region.
   growth ....

When do I use *when*, *if* and *whether*?

1 Tick the correct sentence in each pair.

1 a Many people would stop using their cars when public transport was better.
   b Many people would stop using their cars if public transport was better.
2 a We discussed if universities should charge tuition fees.
   b We discussed whether universities should charge tuition fees.

We use *when* to talk about an event or situation that we believe will happen:
*I plan to go travelling **when** I finish my studies.* (I expect to finish.)
*Give me a call **when** you arrive at the airport.* (We expect the person to arrive.)

We use *if* to talk about a hypothetical possibility, especially in conditional sentences:
*I **would** only go home **if** it was a real emergency.*
*Give me a call **if** there are any problems.* (Problems are only a possibility.)

We also use *if* in certain polite requests:
*I **would appreciate it if** / **would be grateful if** you could call me back.*
***Would you mind if** I asked you a few questions about the accident?*

We use *whether* where we are considering two possibilities:
*I don't know **whether** to have the beef **or** the lamb.*
*Many students have to get part-time jobs **whether or not** they want to.*

We use *whether* after certain verbs (and nouns) which involve considering two options:
*They had a meeting to **discuss whether** they should take further action.*
*The current **debate** is **whether** immigrants should adopt local customs.*

2 Correct the mistake below.

The big question is that I should call him or wait for him to call me.

The big question is ....

3 Complete the sentences using *when*, *if* or *whether*.

1 I'd suggest checking .... the person has a permit or not.
2 We'll probably move to a smaller house .... the children leave home.
3 Why don't you come in the summer .... the weather's better?
4 Some people have questioned .... it's useful or just a waste of money.
5 It would be helpful .... they could give us a breakdown of the marks.
6 They carried out tests to determine .... or not he had the disease.
7 I'm sure they'd be really pleased .... you were able to come.
8 You will need to show your driving licence .... you collect the hire car.

10

5 Punctuation: commas with discourse markers

1 Tick the correct sentence in each pair.

1 a In conclusion, the world population is expanding at an unsustainable rate.
  b In conclusion the world population is expanding at an unsustainable rate.
2 a If we look for example, at sport in schools.
  b If we look, for example, at sport in schools.

Discourse markers are words or phrases which show how ideas in a text link together. They are often separated from the rest of the text by commas.

We usually use a comma after a phrase or an adverb which introduces a sentence:
In addition, many disabled people suffer discrimination at work.
On the other hand, the unemployment rate has fallen.
Finally, local councils need to consider the cost of recycling schemes.
Unfortunately, there were no more tickets available.
Similarly, animals kept outdoors are also vulnerable to infection.

We also use commas around certain words and phrases in the middle of a sentence:
*This problem can't, **however,** be solved quite so simply.*
*There are more jobs in the city, but, **of course,** the cost of living is higher.*
*Which option you choose depends, **to a certain extent,** on your budget.*
*Water is particularly scarce in arid regions, **for example/for instance,** in Africa.*
*People who live in cold countries, **such as/like** Norway, have to spend more on heating.*

☆ Where an adverb describes an adjective, commas are not needed:
*This was matched by a **similarly dramatic** increase in May.*
***However careful** you are, accidents can always happen.*

2 Correct the mistake below.

Inevitably there's always something you forget.

.... something you forget.

3 Add commas in the sentences below where needed.

1 What happens if for example you forget your password?
2 To sum up I'd like to recap the main advantages and disadvantages.
3 Statistics can however be misleading.
4 Low-lying countries such as Bangladesh are particularly at risk.
5 Furthermore not everyone will be able to afford to install new telephones.
6 Contact sports like rugby will inevitably involve more injuries.
7 A similarly priced house in the city centre would only have one bedroom.
8 We will of course reimburse any travel expenses.

6 Punctuation: using apostrophes

1 Tick the correct sentence in each pair.

1 a Many people eat junk food because its easier than preparing fresh dishes.
  b Many people eat junk food because it's easier than preparing fresh dishes.
2 a Please don't take a taxi – I'll come and pick you up.
  b Please dont take a taxi – I'll come and pick you up.

We use an apostrophe in contractions – where a letter or letters have been missed out. Contractions are mostly used in informal writing or to represent spoken language.

Pronoun or noun + *be, have, will* or *would*:
That's (= that is) *a very good point.*
Anna's (= Anna has) *got two sisters, hasn't she?*
We'll (= we will) *send the goods by first class post.*
I'd (= I had) *already gone through passport control, so I couldn't go back.*
I'd (= I would) *like to change the booking.*
It's (= it is) *quite difficult to find.*
☆ *The system has **its** advantages.* (its = belonging to it)
Who's (= who has) *been invited to the party?*
☆ ***Whose** bag is this?* (whose = belonging to who)

Auxiliary or modal verb + *not*:
*The results **haven't** (= have not) been announced yet.*
*I **don't** know the answer.* or *I **do not** know the answer.* (not ~~I donot know the answer.~~)
*They **can't** be copied.* or *They **cannot** be copied.* (not ~~They can not be copied.~~)

Also: ***Let's*** (= let us) *take another example.*

2 Correct the mistake below.

The dog's looking really bored. Where's it's lead? I'll take it for a walk.

The ....? I'll take it for a walk.

3 Add apostrophes where necessary in the sentences below.

1 Its only a matter of time before someones badly injured.
2 You cant always blame parents when their children behave badly.
3 The hotel has its own gym thats free for guests to use at any time.
4 The governments planning to introduce a complete smoking ban.
5 The majority of teenagers dont see healthy eating as a high priority.
6 Lets meet outside the station in the city centre.
7 There isnt much demand for ice cream in the winter.
8 Do you know whos got the key for the store room?

1 **The extracts below from a student essay have a number of commas and apostrophes missing. Add punctuation where necessary.**

The world is facing an energy crisis and undoubtedly one of the keys to tackling this problem is for everyone to use less energy. This solution sounds simple. It isnt however as straightforward as it first seems. ...

Firstly we need to consider the costs for the individual involved in trying to save energy. We could look for example at ways of insulating homes. Many measures such as roof insulation and double-glazing are often expensive to install. Moreover many poor people live in old houses which arent as easy to keep warm as newer buildings. ...

Secondly its much easier for governments of rich countries to introduce regulations for industry without their economies suffering. However for a developing country which is trying to expand its economy, there are much greater risks. ...

In conclusion we can say that we will all have to reduce the amount of energy we use in the future. However important this aim is, though, we need to remember that some will inevitably need help to achieve energy efficiency targets.

2 **Underline the best word or phrase to complete each sentence.**

1 I would be grateful *when/if/whether* you could confirm the booking in writing.
2 What's the best way to deal with a patient *who's/whose/who* behaving aggressively?
3 It's important to start saving towards a pension now so that you're financially secure *if/as/when* you retire.
4 Please don't hesitate to contact me *if/that/whether* you have any questions.
5 I don't know yet *if/that/whether* or not I'll be able to come.
6 Cheap airlines have brought benefits. *Such as/For example/Like*, foreign travel is no longer only for the rich.
7 The bank has announced that it will close 50 of *it's/their/its* 800 branches.
8 MPs will debate *if/about/whether* to change the age limit for buying cigarettes.

3 **Rewrite the sentences below adding the phrase in brackets in an appropriate place. Don't forget any necessary punctuation.**

1 Going by train is slower than flying. (*of course*)
Going by train .... than flying.

2 For many people these rises will cause real difficulties. (*especially single parents*)
For many .... real difficulties.

3 There are alternatives to surgery for some patients. (*however*)
There are .... for some patients.

4 For some people compost bins are not feasible. (*such as those in flats*)
For some .... not feasible.

5 There are a number of precautions we would recommend. (*therefore*)
There are .... recommend.

6 All of us are responsible for cutting emissions. (*to a certain extent*)
All of us .... cutting emissions.

7 Old people are more vulnerable to such infections. (*for instance*)
Old people .... such infections.

8 Such delays are unavoidable. (*unfortunately*)
Such .... unavoidable.

4 **Use the words from the box to complete the advice below. Use one word in each gap and use each word only once.**

when	like	if	whether
however	obviously	its	it's

Considering a gap year abroad?

First, you need to decide (1).......................... you want to spend the year travelling or working in another country. This will, (2).........................., depend partly on your budget.

(3).......................... tempting to just relax and enjoy some time off after all the stress of exams. (4).........................., working in a country will enable you to learn more about (5).......................... people and culture and, ultimately, gain more from the experience. It will also look good on your CV (6).......................... you get back!

(7).......................... you do plan to work while you're away, you'll need to check visa and work permit rules for the country you're visiting. For many countries, (8).......................... the US, it's vital to sort out the paperwork before you go. Check our website for more details.

Common spelling mistakes

1 Tick the correct sentence in each pair.

1 a We have become very dependant on computers.
  b We have become very dependent on computers.
2 a You need to have a clear idea of what you want to achieve.
  b You need to have a clear idea of what you want to acheive.

Nouns which are commonly misspelt include:
accommodation, benefit, country, environment, government, percentage, proportion

In British English, the noun **programme** has two main meanings:
a training **programme** = a series of sessions; *a TV* **programme** = a TV broadcast
But: *a* **computer program** = computer software

Words containing the *ie* or *ei* vowel combination often cause problems. British children learn a rhyme to help them remember: "**I** before **E** except after **C**."
achieve/achievement, believe/belief, hygiene/hygienic, retrieve/retrieval
But: *receive/receipt, deceive/deceit, ceiling*

In British English, *practice* is the spelling of the noun and *practise* is the verb form:
Now they can put into **practice** *what they have learnt.*
It'll be a good opportunity to **practise** *speaking English.*

The adjectives *dependent* and *independent* are spelt with *-ent* at the end:
The degree of influence is **dependent on** *a number of factors.*
Dependant is a noun referring to a person who depends on someone else financially:
The company provides private healthcare for workers and their **dependants**.

2 Correct the mistake below.

I think you need more practise before you take your test.

I think you need ....

3 Correct any spelling errors in the sentences below.

1 I beleive that successful companies need an experienced workforce.
2 We need to look at goverment expenditure on enviromental projects.
3 Food hygine is a major concern for restaurant owners.
4 Many farmers are dependent on foreign investors.
5 This money should be spent to benifit the poorest countaries.
6 Strong health and educational programes are vital for developing nations.
7 The propotion of women who acheive first class degrees is comparatively low.
8 Everyone has the right to practise their religion.

15

8 Spelling: one word or two?

1 Tick the correct sentence in each pair.

1 a More than 20% of the work force is unemployed.
  b More than 20% of the workforce is unemployed.
2 a There are alot of artists living in this district.
  b There are a lot of artists living in this district.

Compounds which are written as one word include:
- *countryside, hairstyle, lifespan, lifestyle, website, wildlife, workforce, workplace*
- *misuse, outbreak, outcome, outside, overall, overcome*
- *anybody, everyone, everything, someone, sometimes*
- *furthermore, moreover, nowadays, throughout, whereas*

Compounds which are written with a hyphen include:
- *make-up, well-being*
- *twenty-four, thirty-five,* etc.

Phrases which are written as separate words include:
- *Young people often spend **a lot** of money on clothes.*
- ***In fact**, levels of pollution have decreased in the past five years.*
- *She still smokes, **even though** she knows it's bad for her health.*

☆ ***Maybe** his plane has been delayed.* (= an adverb meaning *perhaps*)
*I suspect the main reason for the change **may be** financial.* (= a verb phrase)

2 Correct the mistake below.

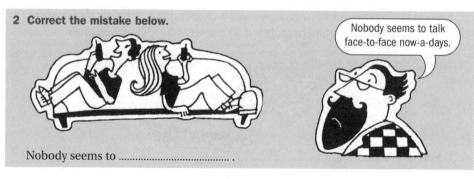

Nobody seems to talk face-to-face now-a-days.

Nobody seems to ....

3 Correct any errors in the compounds and phrases in the sentences below.

1 80% of women said they were satisfied, where as only 60% of men were happy.
2 The room was clean and every thing was neatly arranged.
3 Many of the problems are due to changes in lifestyle.
4 Our main concern is for the health and well being of all our residents.
5 They fled the country just before the outbreak of the civil war.
6 He carried out research into the life-span of people living in the country side.
7 May be learning a foreign language in school should be compulsory.
8 The charity runs twenty six hostels spread through out the country.

16

Adjective forms

1 Tick the correct sentence in each pair.

1 a Many university students have a part-time job.
  b Many university students have a part time job.
2 a These jobs cannot be done by unexperienced young people.
  b These jobs cannot be done by inexperienced young people.

There are many compound adjectives in English which are usually hyphenated:
- *good-looking, good-natured, well-known, well-educated, well-paid, well-equipped*
- *badly-behaved, bad-tempered, ill-equipped, hard-working, easy-going*
- *short-lived, short-tempered, short-term, long-term, long-lasting*
- *fully-qualified, full-scale, full-size, full-time, part-time, time-consuming, time-saving*

Many phrases describing the age, size or length of something are formed in the same way. When they are used before a noun, they are hyphenated:

a **six-year-old** boy	He is **six years old**.
a **three-month** training course	The course lasts **three months**.
a **two-bedroom** flat	a flat with **two bedrooms**

Adjectives are also formed using prefixes, especially to describe opposites:

dis-	*dissatisfied, disorganised*	**over-**	*overcrowded, overpriced*
in-	*inexpensive, inexperienced, inappropriate*	**post-**	*post-school, postgraduate*
im-	*immoral, immature, impolite*	**pre-**	*pre-school, prearranged*
non-	*nonexistent, non-smoking*	**un-**	*unaware, unsuitable, unemployed*

☆ Some of these adjectives are spelt with a hyphen and some as one word; check a dictionary for the correct spelling.

2 Correct the mistake below.

Don't you think that's a bit unappropriate for a job interview?

Don't you think ....?

3 Underline the correct word.

1 The figure rose steadily over a *30 year/30-year* period.
2 The stalls sell a variety of *non-expensive/inexpensive* snacks.
3 He was a polite, *well-educated/good-educated* man.
4 The family live in a simple, *single-storey/single storeys* house.
5 She is punctual, conscientious and *hard work/hard-working*.
6 Everyone needs a healthy, *well-balanced/well balanced* diet.
7 All supervisors must attend a *week-long/one week long* safety course.
8 Many tourists go into the mountains wearing *insuitable/unsuitable* clothing.

1 The letter below contains 15 mistakes. Find them and correct them.

I am writing to express my unsatisfacation with both the standard of acomodation and the service I recieved during a recent visit to your hotel.

I had booked a not-smoking doubleroom for two nights from 15th April. However, when I arrived, I was told by a rather unpolite receptionist that there was only a single room available. I then found that it was a fifth floor room and the lift was autoforder. Eventhough I had a number of heavy bags, no body offered to help me.

More over, when I arrived at my room, I realised that I had been given the uncorrect key and had to return to the reception desk. When I finally found some one to exchange the key and managed to get into my room, I found that it was cramped and illequipped, with no phone or television as advertised on your web-site.

2 Rewrite the sentences using an adjective + noun to replace the underlined phrase.

Example:

His parents both have <u>jobs that pay well</u>.

His parents both have ....*well-paid jobs*.....

1 The exhibition featured a number of <u>devices that can save you time</u>.
   The exhibition featured a number of ....
2 All the chalets have <u>kitchens with all the equipment you need</u>.
   All the chalets have ....
3 My grandfather was <u>a man with a rather short temper</u>.
   My grandfather was ....
4 We stayed in <u>a castle which was built 200 years ago</u>.
   We stayed in ....
5 Fighting has resumed after <u>a ceasefire which lasted for a short while</u>.
   Fighting has resumed after ....
6 The man <u>was sentenced to 5 years in prison</u>.
   The man received ....

3 Underline the correct words in the text below.

Stayfit

The Stayfit Health Club offers a wide range of fitness (1) *programs/programmes* to suit your (2) *life-style/lifestyle*. Choose from a package of individual sessions with one of our (3) *fully-trained/full-trained* instructors or join in with any of the (4) *twenty-five/twenty five* different exercise classes we run each week. Alternatively, you can brush up on your serves or (5) *practice/practise* your backhands on our (6) *full-size/full size* indoor tennis courts.

Apply now for a 20% discount* on a
(7) *12 months/12-month* membership package.

*Availability (8) *dependent/dependant* on demand.

4 The printer has forgotten to add spaces and punctuation to the personal ads below. Rewrite them with appropriate spaces between words and any necessary punctuation.

1
> goodlookingeasygoing
> 30yearoldmanseekswell
> educatedyoungwoman

2
> attractivewellequippedtwobedroo
> mholidaycottagesetinbreathtakingc
> ountrysidenonsmokersonlyplease

3
> treatyourselftoaonetooneconsultationwithoneofo
> urfullyqualifiedbeautytherapistsforprofessionalad
> viceonyourmakeupandhairstyle

4
> fedupwithovercrowdedoverpricedresortswhynottryaweekend
> breakinsofiacheckourwebsitefordetailsofinexpensivetwoday
> breaksinbulgariashistoriccapital

10 Using prepositions: with nouns

1 Tick the correct sentence in each pair.

1 a Many newspaper articles are also available on the internet now.
  b Many newspaper articles are also available through the internet now.
2 a There are three main reasons of this change.
  b There are three main reasons for this change.

We use the preposition *on* to talk about information or pictures we access or see using a computer or other screen, such as a television:
*You can easily check the train times **on the internet**.*
*More information is available **on** the university **website**.*
*You can download music and store it **on** your **computer**.*
*We see such scenes every night **on** the TV news.*

We often use the preposition *for* with the noun *reason*:
*a reason for something: No one explained the **reason for** the delay.*
*a reason for doing something: There are many **reasons for** choosing a small car.*
*for a reason: He was forced to leave early **for** family **reasons**.*

Due to is also used to introduce a reason for something. *Due to* already contains the idea of a reason, so we do not use *due to + a reason*:
The flight was delayed due to technical problems.
or *The flight was delayed for technical reasons.*
not ~~The flight was delayed due to technical reasons.~~

2 Correct the mistake below.

> According to a statement in his website, he left the club for personal reasons.

According to a statement ....

3 Use the words below (in the same order) to create sentences. Add any necessary prepositions or articles, and put the verbs in an appropriate form.

1 Young people / copy / role models / they / see / television
2 Band / cancel / performance / personal / reasons
3 Building / closed / public / safety concerns
4 Prime Minister / appear / last night / BBC current affairs programme
5 She / not / give / reason / be / late
6 Many people / now / book / holidays / internet
7 They / spend / eight hours / day / work / computer
8 Then / error message / suddenly / appear / screen

Using prepositions: after verbs

1 Tick the correct sentence in each pair.

1 a Companies in the US spend more money on research and development.

b Companies in the US spend more money for research and development.

2 a We have to provide doctors with the resources they need to do their job.

b We have to provide doctors the resources they need to do their job.

There are a number of common verb + object + preposition combinations in English. You can check the patterns used with a particular verb in a good learner's dictionary:

- *spend + time/money + on something*
  *The average person **spends** £100 a month **on** transport.*
  Also: ***Expenditure on/Spending on** education has risen.*
- *invest + money + in something*
  *It's up to local government to **invest** money **in** improved leisure facilities.*
  Also: *The protesters want more state **investment in** agriculture.*
- *provide + something + for someone*
  *The project will **provide** employment **for** young artists and performers.*
  Also: *There has been progress in **the provision of** facilities **for** the disabled.*
- *provide + someone + with something*
  *We aim to **provide** the children **with** an opportunity to experience a different culture.*
- *help + someone + (out) + with something*
  *She visits twice a week to **help** her grandmother out **with** the housework.*
  Also: *Some students need extra **help with** reading and writing.*

2 Correct the mistake below.

On average, how much ....?

On average, how much do you spend a month for hair products?

3 There is one incorrect or missing preposition in each sentence below. Make any changes or additions necessary to correct the sentences.

1 Some companies spend huge sums in advertising.

2 The new labels provide customers better information about ingredients.

3 I have a problem I think you can help me.

4 The party promised to increase investment for education.

5 We are pressing for the provision more special lanes for cyclists.

6 There are no facilities provided to passengers with young children.

7 Spending for photographic film has dropped dramatically.

8 There's a porter in reception to help guests their bags.

12 Using prepositions: describing trends and changes

1 Tick the correct sentence in each pair.

1 a There has been an increase in the number of people aged over eighty.
 b There has been an increase of the number of people aged over eighty.
2 a Between 1990 and 2000, there was a drop 15%.
 b Between 1990 and 2000, there was a drop of 15%.

We use a noun describing a specific trend or change + *in* + a word or phrase describing the thing which has changed:
- *a(n) cut/decline/decrease/drop/fall/increase/reduction/rise, etc. in something*
 *The chart shows **a decline in** the bird population.*
 *There have been dramatic **cuts in** the level of spending on the elderly.*
- *a(n) change/growth/improvement/trend/variation, etc. in something*
 *There have been significant **improvements in** health care.*
 *We have seen massive **changes in** people's lifestyles.*

We use a noun describing a change or the result of a change + *of* + a number showing the size of the change:
- *a(n) decrease/drop/fall/increase/reduction/rise, etc. of + number*
 *The statistics show **a reduction of** 20% **in** energy costs as a result of the measures.*
 *The radio station experienced **a fall of** 36,000 listeners to a total audience of 2.1 million.*
- *a high/low/maximum/peak/total, etc. of + number*
 *Demand reached **a peak of** 45,000 in early March.*

2 Correct the mistake below.

The hot weather led to a sudden surge of ice cream sales.

The hot weather led to ....

3 Underline the correct preposition in each sentence.

1 There has been a slight rise *in/of/to* the number of men employed.
2 Experts expect there to be a fall *by/of/in* approximately 30% over the next decade.
3 The introduction of DVDs has led to a decline *of/in/to* video sales.
4 We have seen an increase *by/of/in* only 0.5% during the past year.
5 Researchers observed changes *of/to/in* educational levels.
6 The survey hopes to track trends *for/in/to* consumer spending.
7 The health service spent a total *in/of/at* £2.5 billion on staffing last year.
8 The new figures show a drop of 5% *in/of/to* student numbers.

1 Complete the news stories below with one preposition in each space.

The number of births in Scotland has risen to its highest level since 1999, according to the Registrar General. Figures suggest that more than 54,000 babies were born in 2005, a rise (1) .... 420 births on the previous year – that's an increase (2) .... less than 1%. The increase (3) .... births is lower than the increase (4) .... almost 3% between 2003 and 2004. The Registrar General for Scotland said: "The recent upturn (5) .... the birth rate is encouraging but it may be easing off."

There was a slight decline (6) .... the number of deaths in 2005, with a drop (7) .... the incidence of strokes and heart disease, two of Scotland's top three causes of death. There was also a fall (8) .... the number of both marriages and divorces.

Schools spend much more (9) .... computer-based resources than (10) .... books, new figures suggest. Expenditure (11) .... ICT (information and communication technology) has seen a rise (12) .... more than 50% over the past year, according to figures from the Department of Education. A spokesperson pointed out that one of the reasons (13) .... this shift is that pupils now have more reading material available to them (14) .... the internet. Government figures also show that schools spent £197 million (15) .... exam fees during the same period, a rise (16) .... a quarter in two years.

2 There are 10 mistakes with prepositions in the paragraph below – either incorrect or missing prepositions. Find the mistakes and correct them.

In the past few years, there has been a dramatic increase of the number of budget airlines which offer cheap flights throughout Europe. If you look in the internet, you will find some amazing deals at their websites. These 'no frills' airlines provide very few facilities their passengers, but when they're only spending a few euros for a flight, most people are happy with a basic service. This reduction of the cost of European air travel has, inevitably, led to an explosion of the number of people who can afford to take foreign holidays. The growth to air travel and changes to patterns of tourism within Europe have had both positive and negative impacts. It has encouraged investment for many regional airports and boosted local economies, but what of the environmental impact of those extra air miles?

3 Rewrite the sentences below using the noun form of the underlined verb.

Example:

The graph shows that sales have <u>fallen</u> by 8%.

The graph shows a fall of 8% in sales.

1 We hope to <u>reduce</u> the number of injuries by 25%.
   We hope to achieve a ....
2 The availability of this treatment <u>varies</u> a great deal from one region to another.
   There is ....
3 House prices have <u>risen</u> by 40% in the past five years.
   In the past five years, there has been ....
4 Daytime temperatures can <u>peak</u> at around 30°C in summer.
   Daytime temperatures can ....
5 The new principal is promising to <u>improve</u> computer access for students.
   The new principal is promising ....
6 We need to <u>invest</u> more money in staff training.
   There needs to be ....

4 Below are comments from five people who have chosen to give up their cars, but their words are in the incorrect order. Rewrite them to form correct sentences.

1 giving environmental for My car main reason up my was.

2 mean local I transport need Improvements don't public that just in a car.

3 different for to I rid reasons decided get my car a of number of.

4 economic It fuel to a car any more run due the high wasn't cost to of.

5 money much I spending found on I was too repairs.

Describing statistics: using prepositions

1 Tick the correct sentence in each pair.

1 a The chart shows that only 18% men work less than 15 hours a week.

  b The chart shows that only 18% of men work less than 15 hours a week.

2 a If we look at the figures for people between 20 and 30 years old, ...

  b If we look at the figures for people between 20 to 30 years old, ...

There are several key prepositions which are used when describing statistics:

- *X% **of** something*
  *Only 28% **of** customers said that they were satisfied with the service.*
- ***between** X **and** Y*
  *The rate rose dramatically **between** July 2005 **and** February 2006.*
- *the figure/percentage/total, etc. **for** a group or category*
  *Looking at the figures **for** winter and summer ...*
  *If we compare the percentages **for** skilled and unskilled workers ...*
  *The average income **for** government employees is ...*
- ***at** a level/rate*
  *Inflation has remained **at** roughly the same **level** over a number of years.*
  *They can obtain loans **at** cheaper **rates**.*
- *be highest / come top / rank second, etc. **with** X*
  *Football scored **highest with** 68% of the vote.*
  *Paris is **second** in the table **with** 76 million passengers per year.*

2 Correct the mistake below.

80% dogs
said they preferred
Woofies

80% ....

3 Are these sentences right or wrong? Correct those with mistakes.

1 France has the greatest number at 12 million, followed by Italy.

2 The percentage fluctuated between 3.5 to 4%.

3 The total value is approximately 18,000 yen from the current exchange rate.

4 Data is only available of the UK.

5 The drop-out rate reached a peak of 18% in 2001.

6 The table shows the annual usage for families in three income bands.

7 Africa was the least popular destination by only 6% of flights.

8 12% interviewees had consulted a doctor in the previous week.

14 Describing statistics: nouns

1 Tick the correct sentence in each pair.

1 a Only four percentage of prisoners are women.
   b Only four percent of prisoners are women.
2 a The pie chart illustrates how electricity is used.
   b The pie graph illustrates how electricity is used.

We use *percent* or the symbol % after a number:
*Sales fell by **two percent / 2%** last year.*
Percentage is the general noun to describe part of a total, expressed as parts of 100:
*The chart shows **the percentage of** households with more than one car.*
Proportion is also used to describe part of a total:
*Which country has **the** highest **proportion of** people living in poverty?*
Rate describes how often or how fast something happens, and some other measures:
***The rate of** growth is slower in developing countries.*
Also: *the unemployment/crime rate, the birth/death rate, the exchange/interest rate*

A *graph* has two lines (the *vertical axis* and the *horizontal axis*)
marked with numbers, and a line or curve showing a trend.
A *chart* shows statistics in a visual form, often as coloured lines
or columns (a *bar chart*) or as sections of a circle (a *pie chart*).
A *table* shows something, usually numbers, organised within a
box in *rows* (going across ↔) and *columns* (going down ↕).
A *diagram* is a general word for something represented in a
visual form – for example, showing how something works,
the stages of a process, etc.

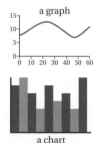

a graph

a chart

---

2 Correct the mistake below.

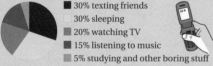

■ 30% texting friends
  30% sleeping
■ 20% watching TV
■ 15% listening to music
■ 5% studying and other boring stuff

The pie chart shows proportion of an average day a student spends on different activities.

The pie chart shows .... a student spends on different activities.

3 Underline the best word to complete each sentence.

1 The figures show the *rate/percentage* of flights delayed by more than 60 minutes.
2 The chart shows the *unemployment/unemployed* rates in six European countries.
3 The *diagram/chart* illustrates the planned layout of the buildings.
4 The operation has a seventy *percentage/percent* success rate.
5 The USA has the highest *proportion/rate* of people aged 65 and over.
6 Some people argue that violent films increase the *criminal/crime* rate.
7 The *percentage/percent* of over 50s who own a mobile phoned has increased.
8 The vertical axis of the *graph/pie chart* shows the number of hours per day.

15 Describing statistics: verbs

1 Tick the correct sentence in each pair.

1 a The birth rate has reduced over the past ten years.
  b The birth rate has dropped over the past ten years.
2 a The graph shows a rise in the number of accidents involving cyclists.
  b The graph represents a rise in the number of accidents involving cyclists.

Common verbs used to describe graphs, charts and diagrams include:
*The chart/graph **shows** levels of post-school education in four countries.*
*The diagram **illustrates/represents** the structure of the political system.*
*The chart/graph **compares** average working hours in the UK and the US.*
***We can see** from the chart/graph **that** the number of visitors peaks in August.*

Common verbs used to describe figures and statistics include:
*The statistics/figures **suggest that** people in rural areas are healthier.*
*The figure will increase further, **reaching** 6 million in 2020. (not ~~touching 6 million~~)*
*Demand **rose** by 48% in just 2 years. (not ~~raised by 48%~~)*
*Time spent with the family **dropped** from 21% to just 6%. (not ~~reduced from 21%~~)*
☆ Verbs such as *rise, drop, decline* and *fall* describe a change which happens.
A person or organisation can *raise* or *reduce* something:
*The Bank of England has **raised** interest rates.*
*The Government has introduced measures to **reduce** traffic in the capital.*

2 Correct the mistake below.

The number of visitors touches a peak in July.

The number of visitors ....

3 Complete the sentences using an appropriate verb.

1 The population of the city .... to a high of 2.3 million in 1997.
2 From the chart, we can .... that expenditure on IT has increased rapidly.
3 The inflation rate has .... its lowest point in 10 years.
4 The chart .... the amount of water consumed per person in each area.
5 Diagram 2.4 .... the life cycle of a butterfly.
6 The results of the survey .... that most people are dissatisfied with public transport.
7 The percentage of households without a phone .... from 23% to just 4%.
8 To combat global warming, we all need to .... the amount of energy we consume.

TEST 5

1 Complete the texts about the charts and graphs using words from the box. Each word is used once.

see	fell	compares	graph	drops	bar chart	rate
in	percent	with	for	comes	pie chart	percentage

The (1) .... above (2) .... the average life expectancy (3) .... men and women living in different areas. We can (4) .... that women in suburban areas have the highest life expectancy, (5) .... an average of 84 years. Life expectancy for both men and women (6) .... significantly for those living in city centres.

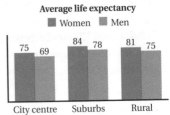

Average life expectancy
■ Women ■ Men

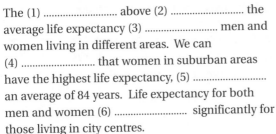

City centre   Suburbs   Rural

The (7) .... shows a slight rise (8) .... the exchange (9) .... in the second quarter. It then (10) .... back to previous levels towards the end of the year.

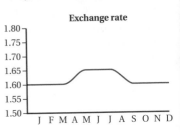

Exchange rate

According to the (11) ...., around a third of the water we use is flushed down the toilet. A fairly large (12) .... of our water usage goes on washing and cleaning. Then showering (13) .... next, accounting for around 28 (14) .... of our daily consumption.

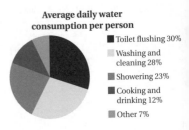

Average daily water consumption per person
■ Toilet flushing 30%
■ Washing and cleaning 28%
■ Showering 23%
■ Cooking and drinking 12%
■ Other 7%

2 Replace any incorrect prepositions or add prepositions where necessary in the sentences below.

1 Numbers dropped dramatically between 2000 to 2005.
2 There are shortages of language teachers in all levels.
3 The graph shows the average rates of pay in workers in four key industries.
4 Women occupy only 5% senior posts in the banking sector.
5 London University came top in the survey at a 75% approval rating.
6 What proportion the overall budget is spent on training?
7 Sea levels are estimated to be rising in a rate of 1.8mm per year.
8 The research compared the data of London, Paris and New York.
9 Three-quarters customers spent $10 or less.
10 The chart shows rates in pay in urban and rural areas.

3 Use the notes below to write complete sentences, keeping the information in the same order. Write out any symbols or abbreviations in full as words.

Example:

water slide = least popular ride – only 2% visitors

The water slide was the least popular ride, with only two percent of visitors.

1 chart shows % employees work late approx. 3 days/week
2 figures show average no. days holiday skilled & unskilled workers
3 rate tooth decay dropped 10% 1980–1990
4 we can see $\frac{2}{3}$ children watch more than 4hrs TV/day
5 Zurich = 2nd in table most expensive European cities
6 1st graph compares % single-parent families different income groups

4 Vocabulary extension. There are many different words used to describe statistics in English. Use a dictionary if necessary to put the words in the box in the correct column below.

dramatically	jump	halve	rapid	plummet
downturn	trough	steep	peak	slump
gradually	sharp	soar	surge	steady
boost	gain	shrink	rocket	diminish

Words to describe a movement or trend upwards ↗ (*nouns and verbs*)	Words to describe a movement or trend downwards ↘ (*nouns and verbs*)	Words to describe a slow change (*adjectives and adverbs*)	Words to describe a fast change (*adjectives and adverbs*)

29

16 Number and *amount*

1 Tick the correct sentence in each pair.

1 a The internet is becoming accessible to a growing amount of people.
   b The internet is becoming accessible to a growing number of people.
2 a The table shows the number of people who visited the gallery each day.
   b The table shows number of people who visited the gallery each day.

We use *number of* before a plural countable noun:
*The chart shows the **number of** hours/passengers/people/schools/times*, etc.

We use *amount of* before an uncountable noun:
*If we look at the **amount of** energy/food/information/money/time/waste, etc … .*

We use *the + number of/amount of* to talk generally about a quantity:
***The number of** passengers carried each year has risen gradually.*
*We need to reduce **the amount of** water we waste.*

We often use *a/an* before an adjective + *number of/amount of*:
*They spend **a significant amount of** money on travel.* (not ~~an important amount of~~)
*This is the best way to reach **a large number of** people.* (not ~~a big number of~~)
But: *the average/greatest/largest/maximum/same/total number/amount of something*

Number and *amount* are used to describe the actual quantities of things or people. *Percentage, proportion, rate*, etc. are used to describe measurements as part of a total:
The percentage of students with blue eyes is 25%.
The number of students with blue eyes is 6.

Eye colour
■ 55% Brown
■ 25% Blue
  15% Green
■ 5% Other

Students in
the group = 24

2 Correct the mistake below.

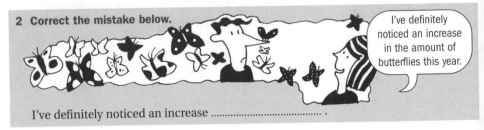

I've definitely noticed an increase in the amount of butterflies this year.

I've definitely noticed an increase ....

3 Add *number of* or *amount of* to the words in italics. Also add articles (*the/a/an*).

1 Which country has *lowest people* living in poverty?
2 People were asked about *time* they spend doing different activities.
3 We looked at *customers* who were attracted into the shop by special offers.
4 The research compared *leisure time* spent with friends and with family members.
5 Such projects can generate *large money* for the tourism industry.
6 Statistics also show *total overseas students* at UK universities has risen.
7 They measured *average times* an employee checks their email per hour.
8 They're being asked to do *same work* in shorter hours.

Making comparisons

1 Tick the correct sentence in each pair.

1 a The rate of union membership rose to 26.2%, comparing to 25.8% last year.
   b The rate of union membership rose to 26.2%, compared to 25.8% last year.
2 a The figure is now three times higher as compare to 1965.
   b The figure is now three times higher than in 1965.

There are a number of common words and phrases that we use to make comparisons:
- *compare* something (*to/with* something)
  *The graph **compares** the crime rates in Japan and the US.*
  *It's impossible to **compare** modern films **with** those made maybe 20 years ago.*
  *Many have **compared** her voice **to** Aretha Franklin's.* (= they have said it is similar)
- *compared to/with* something
  *Women's income rose by 31% **compared to** only 13% for men.* (not ~~comparing to~~)
- *in comparison* (*to/with* something)
  *US workers get very little holiday **in comparison with** their European counterparts.*
  *After two weeks in a tent, the simple little hotel seemed luxurious **in comparison**.*
- (*draw/make*) *a comparison between* two things
  ***There is no comparison between** my life here **and** the way of life in my home village.*
  *It is impossible to **draw a** direct **comparison between** the two conflicts.*
- something is *bigger/higher/lower/more important*, etc. *than* something else
  *Prague has **more** churches **than** any other European city.*
- something is *double/half*, etc. *that of* something else
  *Britain's population density is **double that of** China.* (not ~~compared to~~)

2 Correct the mistake below.

Fifi's really quite big as compare with my last dog.

Fifi's really quite big ....

3 Are the sentences right or wrong? Correct those which are wrong.

1 66.6 million people travelled abroad in 2007, comparing to 64.6 million in 2006.
2 Non-smokers' risk of heart attacks is roughly half that of people who smoke.
3 In comparative with other writers, she uses very simple, everyday language.
4 There is no comparison to watching a band on DVD and seeing them play live.
5 The pass rate was over 70% in 2005, compare to 62% in 1990.
6 Many more crimes were committed by males compared to females.
7 The article draws a comparison between his writing and that of earlier authors.
8 Population growth is quite high in Madagascar at 3.31% when compaired to
   Mauritius at 0.89%.

18 Expressing contrast

1 Tick the correct sentence in each pair.

1. a Germany spent 1.5% of GDP on defence. The US, in contrast, spent 3.2%.
   b Germany spent 1.5% of GDP on defence. On the contrary, the US spent 3.2%.
2. a Japan, on the other hand, experienced a slight drop over the same period.
   b Japan, on the other side, experienced a slight drop over the same period.

We use *in contrast* to introduce a fact or idea which is very different from what has already been mentioned. Notice the position of the phrase in the sentence:
*Questionnaires produce only limited responses. Interviews, **in contrast**, are time-consuming, but allow for fuller replies.*
*In Britain only 9% of over sixties live with their families, **in contrast to** 29% in Japan.*
We can also say that there is *a contrast between* two things which are very different:
*There is a stark **contrast between** the affluent suburbs **and** the nearby slum areas.*

We use *on the contrary*, especially in speech, to introduce the opposite of what has just been said or to express an opposite opinion:
'Have visitor numbers dropped since the attack?' 'On the contrary, they've risen slightly.'

We use the phrase *on the other hand* to introduce an opposite viewpoint:
*Parents need to warn their child about things to avoid, but, **on the other hand**, they must not make the child over-anxious.*

2 Correct the mistake below.

I'm a bit of a fitness fanatic. My sister, on the contrary, prefers less energetic hobbies.

I'm a bit of a fitness fanatic. My sister ....

3 Complete the sentences with one of the phrases from above.

1. Abacus made profits of $343 million. Zenon, ..., made only $17.9 million.
2. Water doesn't shrink when it turns into ice, but, ..., it expands.
3. The town remains relatively undeveloped .... others along the coast.
4. The .... the two politicians could not be greater.
5. A dog's nose is vastly more sensitive than our own. Birds, ..., have a comparatively poor sense of smell.
6. The centre of the island is wild and rocky .... the soft sandy beaches.
7. Overweight people usually clear their plate. Slim people, ..., stop eating when they feel satisfied.
8. Some jobs might be lost, but ...., others would be created.

1 Underline the best words or phrases to complete the text below.

Does the (1) *amount/number* of time you spend in bed affect your performance in the office? According to a recent survey, insomniacs miss an average of 5.8 days a year from work. Good sleepers, (2) *on the contrary/in contrast*, miss only 2.4 days on average. This chart (3) *contrasts/compares* the average (4) *number/proportion* of hours sleep a night for people in different professions. Mechanics get the most sleep, with 7.6 hours per night, (5) *in contrast to/in contrast* doctors and company directors, who

Average hours of sleep a night

Doctors	5.6
Company directors	5.8
Emergency services	6.2
Nurses	6.3
Housewives	6.5
Retail staff	6.9
Government workers	7.0
Mechanics	7.6

sleep for less than 6 hours. Shift workers such as nurses and members of the emergency services, unsurprisingly, get relatively little sleep (6) *in comparison with/comparing to* those in nine-to-five jobs. How stressful your job is could also affect the (7) *amount/number* of sleep you get, with one in five insomniacs blaming work pressures for their sleeplessness. The figures suggest that government employees are good sleepers (8) *compared to/compares to* private sector workers, so perhaps job security plays a role as well.

2 Match the two halves of the sentences.

1 The sample contained an equal number of   damage to the environment.
2 They are expected to make a certain number of   space available.
3 The job involves a fair amount of   players in each team.
4 There is only a limited amount of   boys and girls.
5 We try to cause the minimum amount of   travelling.
6 There are the same number of   calls per hour.

3 Rewrite the sentences using the word in brackets without changing it.

1 Spain has a relatively low crime rate compared with other European countries.
   (*comparison*) Spain has ....
2 The average life expectancy of someone living in Mozambique is only 31 years compared with 78 years in the UK, 79 in France and nearly 81 in Japan.
   (*contrast*) The average life expectancy of someone living in Mozambique is only 31 years ....
3 Mountain biking and track cycling are completely different.
   (*no comparison*) There ....
4 Many people have compared them to the Beatles.
   (*comparison*) Many people have ....
5 Most European students receive some funding. In the USA, however, students work their way through college.
   (*hand*) Most European students receive some funding. ....

4 Edit the excerpts below, correcting any mistakes.

> Taxpayers in Belgium pay a large proportion of their income in tax in comparison between other EU countries. The average worker pays 55.6% of their income in tax comparing with only 29.7% in the UK. The proportion paid by Irish workers is only 25.8%, that's almost half compared to workers in Germany.

> London stands out from other parts of the UK in several respects. It has by far the greatest population density with an average of 4,726 people per square kilometre in 2004. On the contrary, Scotland has the lowest population density, with only 65 people per square kilometre. Compared between those living in other regions, people in London are more likely to live alone. London is also home to the highest amount of people from non-white ethnic groups – 29 percent of its population, compared with 8 percent for the UK as a whole.

5 Choose the best adjective from the box to complete the sentences. Use each word only once. Not all of the adjectives are used.

enormous	low	small	certain	fair	direct	equal
marked	big	same	stark	large	limited	increasing

1 There isn't sufficient detail available for all sectors to make a .... comparison.
2 An .... number of public phones now also accept credit cards.
3 Wanaka's laid-back atmosphere stands in .... contrast to the bustle of nearby Queenstown.
4 There are only a .... number of places still available.
5 A standard measure of wine, spirit or beer contains the .... amount of alcohol – 100ml.
6 A .... comparison is only possible where all the external factors are the same.
7 They were not equipped to cope with such a .... number of people.
8 The film has generated an .... amount of media interest.
9 The top fifth of families received 47 percent of the total income. The lowest fifth, in .... contrast, received 3.4 percent.
10 The building work is bound to cause a .... amount of disruption.

Countable and uncountable nouns

1 Tick the correct sentence in each pair.

1 a International aid is very important after natural disasters.
   b International aids are very important after natural disasters.
2 a Every country has its own customs and behaviours.
   b Every country has its own customs and behaviour.

Many common nouns in English are uncountable – they do not have a plural form and they are followed by a singular verb form. These include: *aid, behaviour, clothing, employment, equipment, furniture, help, information, pollution, software, transport:*
A lot of information is *available on the internet.*

Nouns ending *-ing* to describe an activity are also uncountable: *advertising, farming, shopping, swimming, training,* etc.:
*This type of **farming** causes damage to the environment.*

Some words have countable [C] and uncountable [U] forms used in different contexts:
*He has no **work experience**.* (U: knowledge and skills you gain by doing something)
*Going into hospital is often **a stressful experience**.* (C: a particular event or situation)
***How much time** do you spend commuting?* (U: hours, minutes, etc.)
***How many times** do you go each week?* (C: occasions)
*The waiters all wear **local dress**.* (U: clothes for a particular context)
*She had two bridesmaids in pink **dresses**.* (C: a piece of women's clothing)
Also: *We often go walking in **the country**.* (singular: the countryside)
      *He's visited a number of **countries**.* (C: a nation)

2 Correct the mistake below.

I didn't know we were meant to come in evening dresses.

I didn't know we ....

3 Underline the correct word in each sentence.

1 The shop sells children's *clothings/clothing* and footwear.
2 In developing *countries/country*, malaria still kills millions each year.
3 She has 20 years of *experiences/experience* as a nurse.
4 The company sells specialist *softwares/software* for computer-aided design.
5 These patients need injections several *times/time* a day.
6 It has excellent facilities, with all the latest *equipments/equipment*.
7 Cigarette *advertisings/advertising* has been banned in many countries.
8 How often do you use public *transports/transport*?

20 Singular and plural verb forms

1 Tick the correct sentence in each pair.

1 a Health and education are top priorities for the new government.
  b Health and education is top priority for the new government.
2 a The number of students going on to higher education has increased.
  b The number of students going on to higher education have increased.

We use a singular verb form (*is, has, makes, needs,* etc.):

- after a singular noun
  *Each **team has** eleven players.*
  ***Everybody needs** a minimum amount of sleep per night.*
- after an uncountable noun
  ***Research shows** that people with pets are less likely to suffer from stress.*
- after the *number/percentage/proportion,* etc. *of*
  ***The proportion of** people living alone **has** increased.*

We use a plural verb form (*are, have, make, need,* etc.):

- after a plural noun
  *Most **people recycle** less than 30% of their waste.*
  ***Computers have** become a normal part of everyday life.*
- after two or more singular or uncountable nouns considered together
  ***Japan and the US have** similar rates of literacy.*

☆ Remember that where you use more than one verb in a sentence with the same subject, they must all be in the same form:
***The project provides** a place for children to play safely **and keeps** them out of trouble.*

2 Correct the mistake below.

Small children loves playing with the animals.

Small children ....

3 Complete each sentence with the correct present form of the verb in brackets.

1 New technology .... (*allow*) us to analyse the data in seconds.
2 Older people often .... (*eat*) less and .... (*need*) less sleep.
3 Advances in medicine .... (*mean*) that people are living longer.
4 Access to clean drinking water .... (*be*) a basic human right.
5 Everyone .... (*receive*) a welcome pack on the first day.
6 Fish and meat .... (*be*) both sources of protein.
7 The number of places available .... (*vary*) each year.
8 Mobile phones .... (*have*) changed the way we communicate.

It, they and them

1 Tick the correct sentence in each pair.

1 a There have been big changes in the food we eat and the way we cook them.
  b There have been big changes in the food we eat and the way we cook it.
2 a Such films are not suitable for children because they contain violence.
  b Such films are not suitable for children because it contains violence.

It refers back to a singular or uncountable noun we have mentioned before:
*I've lost **my umbrella**, have you seen **it** anywhere?*
*Emergency **aid** can help in the short term, but **it** isn't the answer in the long term.*
*Each **school** has **its** own computer support officer.*

They refers back to a plural noun when the pronoun is the subject of a verb:
*Such **events** cost a lot of money, but **they** can also create jobs for local people.*
*Don't take these **painkillers** when driving as **they** may cause drowsiness.*

Them refers back to a plural noun when the pronoun is the object of a verb:
***Medical facilities** have to be located where people can make best use of **them**.*

We use *their* before something which belongs to a plural noun:
*We help developing **countries** to manage **their** natural resources carefully.*

☆ We usually only use *he/him* and *she/her* to refer to people and not to things:
*My **car's** quite old, but **it's** still fairly reliable. (not ~~she's~~)*

2 Correct the mistake below.

Tom, don't take all the toys, share it with your sister.

Tom, don't take all the toys, ...

3 Complete the sentences with one pronoun in each space.

1 With a digital camera you can take photos and send .... to your friends.
2 I did all my homework and handed .... in on time.
3 The plane was forced to land when .... developed engine trouble.
4 You should take off your shoes and leave .... outside the temple.
5 If you drink too much coffee, ... can stop you sleeping.
6 Fifty years ago, most women didn't work, ... stayed at home with the children.
7 We need to crack down on illegal drugs and the people who sell ....
8 Such huge companies have a number of advantages over .... competitors.

1 Complete each sentence with one of the nouns from the box. Each word is used only once. Change the form of the noun if necessary.

training	shopping	equipment	behaviour	damage
help	idea	information	country	time

1 Parents should be responsible for the .... of their children.
2 There's more .... available on our website.
3 The fire caused a lot of .... to the school buildings.
4 Helen came up with some interesting .... for fundraising events.
5 Sports such as golf require expensive ....
6 Many people do all their .... at the supermarket.
7 She thanked the volunteers for all their ....
8 All staff receive .... in first aid.
9 I phoned several .... but kept getting the answering machine.
10 Mali is one of the most sparsely populated .... in the world.

2 Edit the essay introductions below. Each paragraph contains 8 errors – find the errors and correct them.

Researches have shown that young children finds it easier to learn languages than teenagers and adults. There is no doubt that learning new languages are more difficult once you are an adult, but they are certainly not impossible. Many people take up a new language later in life and becomes fluent speakers. But what are the best teachings methods for such adult learners?

In many western country, obesity among children are increasing. In the UK, for example, the proportion of overweight children have doubled in the past 10 years. Some people believes that children is getting fatter as a result of eating too much fast foods. Others, however, argue that it is not getting enough exercise.

New technology allow us to access news and other informations online from all over the world. This raises the question whether newspapers is necessary in the modern world or whether it will soon disappear. Despite the availability of news websites which is updated 24 hours a day, newspapers still continues to be printed and people continues to buy it.

3 In the letter below, there are 10 verbs in bold. In each case, underline the noun which is the subject of the verb. Is the verb in the correct form? Correct any which are wrong.

Dear Mohammed,

How are you? I'm getting in touch because I'm planning to come to Egypt on holiday soon and I'd like to ask you for some advice.

I know that a lot of <u>tourists</u> **visits** *visit* Egypt every year, so I'd like to choose a time when the main tourist attractions [1]**is** least crowded. When is the best time? I also know that your country [2]**has** a hot climate. [3]**Are** the weather hot all year round?

I'd be keen to know more about Egyptian customs too. What sort of dress [4]**are** appropriate when you are out in the street? I realise that in many Muslim countries, women [5]**cover** their heads and [6]**wears** clothing which [7]**cover** their arms and legs. Are tourists expected to dress in the same way?

And what about the food? I've heard that Egyptian cooking [8]**use** a lot of spices and many dishes [9]**contains** meat. As I'm a vegetarian, do you think I will have a problem?

Sorry for all my questions. Could you recommend any websites which [10]**has** information about Egyptian culture and customs? Thanks for your help.

Best wishes,

Anna.

---

4 Vocabulary extension. Are these words countable or uncountable? Label them C or U. Use a good learner's dictionary to check if necessary.

computer	advice	hour	aspect	accommodation
nation	potential	job	heating	paperwork

22 Verbs: *being* and *having*

1 Tick the correct sentence in each pair.

1 a Of course, there are some students being more willing to study than others.
  b Of course, there are some students who are more willing to study than others.
2 a In the West, we are used to having clean water which comes out of the tap.
  b In the West, we are used to have clean water which comes out of the tap.

The verbs *be* and *have* are not usually used in continuous forms (*being* and *having*) when they are a main verb with their basic meaning – *be* = to exist, *have* = to possess:
*These people **are** among the most disadvantaged in society.* (not ~~are being~~)
*They **have** a loving family to look after them.* (not ~~are having~~)

They are sometimes used as a main verb with a different meaning in a continuous form to emphasise a temporary state or action:
*She's **having a shower** at the moment – can she call you back?* (= showering)
*We're **having a great time** here in New York.* (= enjoying our visit)
*My boss **is being awkward** about giving me time off.* (= behaving in an awkward way)
☆ *Being* + adjective is only used with adjectives which describe an attitude or behaviour (*honest*, *patient*, etc.), not those describing feelings (*happy*, *sad*, etc.).

Continuous forms can also be used after certain words and phrases, including:
be used to, enjoy, like, look forward to, be advantages to, be worth, a reason for, rather than, without
*I'm not **used to being** away from my family.* (= not accustomed to it)
*There are **advantages to having** a flat in the city centre.*

2 Correct the mistake below.

I'm really looking forward to have a place of my own.

I'm really looking forward ....

3 Complete the sentences with the correct form of *be* or *have*.

1 Japan has a large number of people who .... 65 or over.
2 He enjoys .... the centre of attention.
3 People of my grandmother's generation .... traditional values.
4 There are sometimes disadvantages to .... a vegetarian.
5 When I left the house, he .... his breakfast.
6 Each cottage .... its own kitchen facilities.
7 I don't know how to tell her without .... rude.
8 I think he's looking forward to .... some time off work.

40

Commonly confused verbs: *join/attend, give/provide*

1 **Tick the correct sentence in each pair.**

1 a Some people can't afford to join private language courses.

   b Some people can't afford to attend private language courses.

2 a The university library provides free internet access for students.

   b The university library gives free internet access for students.

We use *join* to talk about becoming a member of something, such as a club:
*I try to stay healthy, so I've **joined** a gym.*

We use *attend* to talk about going regularly to a class, course, school or university:
*We had the chance to **attend** a presentation skills workshop.* (not ~~join~~)
We also *attend* an organised event, such as a conference, meeting or church service:
*The Prime Minister **attended** a memorial service for the victims.*
We usually use *go to* instead of *attend* in more informal writing and speech:
*Are you **going to** this afternoon's lecture?* (not ~~attending~~)

We use *provide* to talk about making something available for people to use. We use it
especially about services supplied by the government, a company or other organisation:
*One of the roles of the state is to **provide** a basic education.*
*We need to **provide** better facilities **for** visitors.*
*The tourist office **provides** visitors **with** helpful information.*

Give is usually used in more informal contexts or when one person physically gives
something to someone else:
*The Red Cross **gave** the most malnourished children high-energy drinks.*

2 Correct the mistake below.

All team members are expected to join daily training sessions.

All team members are expected ....

3 **Underline the best verb to complete the sentences.**

1 All employees have the opportunity to *join/attend* IT training courses.

2 The council should *give/provide* better public services for local residents.

3 He is due to *go/attend* a meeting in Munich tomorrow.

4 You will be *given/provided* a coloured wristband when you arrive.

5 She encouraged workers to *join/attend* the trade union.

6 The university website *gives/provides* information for overseas students.

7 I *went to/attended* a great party on Saturday night.

8 Can you *give/provide* me any information about tourist attractions in the area?

24 Verb collocations

1 Tick the correct sentence in each pair.

1 a They have made a lot of progress in improving working conditions.
 b They have achieved a lot of progress in improving working conditions.
2 a Poor diet in childhood can have a long-term effect on health.
 b Poor diet in childhood can leave a long-term effect on health.

There are many common verb + noun combinations (*collocations*) in English:
make progress: I think the team have made progress this season.
make an impression: It is important to make a good first impression.
make a difference: We believe we can make a difference to children's lives.
make someone/something happy/comfortable/effective, etc.: The system can be improved to make it more effective.
have an effect: This incident will have a negative effect on tourism.
have time: Retired people have more time to spend on their hobbies.
have a(n) advantage/benefit: Tea is believed to have health benefits.
give a(n) reason/explanation: He didn't give any explanation.
give someone a(n) chance/opportunity: Give her a chance to explain first.
deal with a problem/situation: There are several problems we need to deal with.
commit a crime: She proved that he didn't commit the crime.

2 Correct the mistake below.

Can you make me one reason why I should give it back?

Can you .... ?

3 Complete the sentences with an appropriate form of one of the verbs above.

1 His manager agreed to .... him one final chance.
2 The police are trained to .... such emergency situations.
3 I tried restarting the computer, but it didn't .... any difference.
4 There was a rise in the number of violent crimes .... in the city last year.
5 Working mothers often don't .... time to cook fresh meals.
6 Both plans .... their advantages and disadvantages.
7 This new treatment will .... life easier for asthma sufferers.
8 His mother's death .... a profound effect on him.

1 **Underline the best verb to complete the comments below.**

"When I first (1) *attended/joined* the club, obviously, I wanted to
(2) *make/have* a good impression on the coach. I hope that if I train
hard, he'll (3) *give/let* me a chance to play in the first team. But I'm
(4) *be/being* realistic about things – I know it takes time to reach the top."

"My wife's 6 months pregnant and I'm really looking forward to (5) *be/being*
a father. When she first told me she (6) *was having/has* a baby, it was a bit
of a shock; I knew it would (7) *have/make* a huge effect on our lives. But
now I've got used to the idea, I (8) *'m/'m being* really excited about it."

"I was quite surprised when we were (9) *given/provided* our
timetables at the start of term. We only have to (10) *attend/go to*
six lectures a week, so we (11) *have/spend* plenty of time to do
other stuff. The course so far has been really interesting and
quite challenging without (12) *been/being* too tough."

2 **Use the words below in an appropriate form and in the same order to make correct
sentences. Add any necessary articles or prepositions.**

Example:
the children be used to have structure their day
The children are used to having a structure to their day.

1   I usually grab sandwich lunchtime rather than have cooked meal
2   not take room without have look first
3   building have smoke alarms every room
4   he not give reason for be late
5   she be quite shy and she not really like be in the spotlight
6   the young mums enjoy have chat while children play
7   villagers not have access clean water or health care
8   there be advantages be part of organised tour group

3 Edit the text below. There are 10 mistakes involving the form of verbs or choice of verbs. Find them and correct them.

FOREIGN NURSES ~~DO~~ *MAKE* A BAD IMPRESSION ON PATIENTS

Nurses joining their annual conference yesterday called on the Health Service to give better support for nurses recruited from overseas who come to work in the UK.

Although nurses from abroad are being highly trained, they often find that UK hospitals are having different working practices and, in some cases, they are not used to have the same responsibilities.

Also many foreign nurses are not provided proper training in language and cultural differences and they are often not equipped to manage the problems they face with patients. They sometimes don't know how to talk about sensitive issues without to be rude or too direct. Many newly-arrived nurses said that the hints and advice they received from colleagues give a big difference and become it easier to fit in.

4 Check for yourself. Complete the sentences below using the correct form of *make*, *have* or *give*. If necessary, check the underlined noun in a good learner's dictionary to find the correct collocation.

1 I think the department has .... a good <u>start</u> to the year.
2 He didn't .... much <u>success</u> in persuading her to stay.
3 Lots of people .... <u>lunch</u> at their desk, usually just a quick sandwich.
4 It's a good way for children to .... new <u>friends</u>.
5 This sort of behaviour .... the school a bad <u>name</u>.
6 We have some important <u>decisions</u> to .... about the future of the business.
7 My parents .... me a <u>lift</u> to the airport.
8 I'll .... a <u>word</u> with the receptionist about it.
9 George .... a nasty <u>comment</u> about her hair.
10 I'll .... you a <u>ring</u> next week and we can arrange a time to meet.

Commonly confused nouns: *habits*, *customs* and *practices*

1 Tick the correct sentence in each pair.

1 a As a tourist, you should show respect for local behaviour.

 b As a tourist, you should show respect for local customs.

2 a They encourage the practice of teachers reading aloud to young children.

 b They encourage the habit of teachers reading aloud to young children.

A *habit* is something a person does regularly in a particular way as part of their everyday life, often without thinking about it:

*After a while, separating rubbish for recycling just becomes a **habit**.*

*People's **eating habits** have changed. Families no longer eat meals together.*

A *custom* is something people in a particular country or of a particular religious or ethnic group do because it has been part of their culture or way of life for many years:

*He studied Maori culture and **customs**.*

*The **custom of** decorating eggs goes back hundreds of years.*

A *practice* is a method of doing something which is usually used, especially in a particular country, industry, etc. In this sense, *practice* is a countable noun.:

*The report condemned **the practice of** keeping prisoners in chains.*

*Modern **agricultural practices** are to blame for the decline in wild flowers.*

Someone's *behaviour* is the way they behave generally or on a particular occasion. *Behaviour* is usually an uncountable noun and has no plural form:

*The appalling **behaviour of** a minority of fans ruined the event for everyone.*

2 Correct the mistake below.

It is a British habit for a man to carry his new wife into their new home.

It is ....

3 Underline the best noun to complete each of the sentences below.

1 The people of the island are proud of their history and *customs/behaviours*.

2 It is now a common *practice/custom* to allow calculators in maths lessons.

3 Parents need more control over their children's viewing *habits/practice*.

4 In accordance with Muslim *custom/habit*, he was buried within hours of his death.

5 He's picked up some bad *behaviours/habits* from his new friends.

6 We hope to end the *habit/practice* of employing children to work in the mines.

7 It is sometimes difficult to keep local *habits/customs* alive in a global age.

8 Should you reward children for good *behaviour/habit*?

1 Tick the correct sentence in each pair.

1 a Changes to the exam format could have a serious influence on candidates.

b Changes to the exam format could have a serious effect on candidates.

2 a It is difficult to assess the impact of the disaster on tourism.

b It is difficult to assess the extent of the disaster on tourism.

An *influence* is something which causes people to think or behave in a different way:
*We need to learn more about the **influence of** violent computer games **on** young people.*
*Our experiences **have** a huge **influence on** our personality.*

An *effect* is what happens to someone or something as a result of something else:
*Research has shown the harmful **effects of** stress **on** the mother and unborn baby.*
*The new resort has **had** a beneficial **effect on** local businesses.* (not ~~effect to~~)
☆ Remember, *effect* is a noun. The verb form is *affect*:
*Homes on the west coast were most **seriously affected by** the hurricane.*

An *impact* is a powerful effect of something, especially something new, on a person or situation:
*We need to look at the environmental **impact of** the new dam.*
*Recent advances have **had** a massive **impact on** the personal computer industry.*

The word *consequences* is also used to talk about the results, often bad, of an action:
*Children need to be taught about **the consequences of** doing wrong.*
*He believes that the 24–7 society **has** negative **consequences for** family life.*

2 Correct the mistake below.

We're very worried about the effects of transport policy for wildlife.

We're very worried about ....

3 Are these sentences right or wrong? Correct those which are wrong.

1 The working environment can have an effect in the health of the workforce.

2 Water pollution has a particularly harmful influence on fish.

3 We see the impact of religion on dress and customs.

4 The new regulations will have a huge impact on the computer industry.

5 Many people are concerned about the efforts of violent films.

6 Celebrities have to be aware of the influence they make on young people.

7 Alcoholism can have a devastating affect on family life.

8 What is the social impact of such a project?

Commonly confused nouns: time words

1 Tick the correct sentence in each pair.

1 a The effects will only be seen over a long duration.
  b The effects will only be seen over a long period of time.
2 a Managers are expected to work for long time.
  b Managers are expected to work long hours.

We use *hours* to talk about the time during a day or week when something usually happens, especially the time when someone works or when something is open:
working hours   office hours   opening hours
*Most nannies **work long hours** for low pay.* (= they work many hours a day)

We use *period* or *period of time* to talk about a particular length of time:
*Sales rose by 20% over **a six-month period**/over **a period of six months**.*
*Sportsmen can earn a lot of money, but only for **a** relatively **short period of time**.*

We use *duration* in formal writing to talk about how long something lasts:
*Make sure that your visa is valid for **the duration of** your stay.*

The *timing* of something is when it happens within the context of other events:
*He said **the timing of** the announcement is not related to next week's board meeting.*

Time is also used in a number of common expressions:
*How do people spend their **spare time**/**free time**/**leisure time**?*
*We spent **most of the time** on the beach.* (not ~~most of the times~~)
*We haven't seen each other for **a long time**.* (not ~~for long time~~)

2 Correct the mistake below.

Museum Open
10am - 5pm daily
MUSEUM INFORMATION
GUIDE BOOK
Excuse me. Can you tell me the museum timings?

Excuse me. Can you tell me .... ?

3 Complete the sentences using one of the words above in each gap.

1 It will take a long .... to repair all the damage.
2 The rate fell gradually over the .... from 1990 to 2000.
3 Passengers are not permitted to smoke for the .... of the flight.
4 Office .... are from 9.00am to 5.30pm.
5 Many have criticised the .... of the referendum.
6 He spends a lot of his spare .... in the garden.
7 He built up his reputation over a .... of time.
8 We are sometimes asked to work extra .... at weekends.

TEST 9

1 These are all things which British people do. Which are *customs*, *habits* or *practices*? Label them C, H or P.

1 People usually wear black at a funeral.
2 People often drink coffee with their breakfast.
3 Families have a decorated fir tree in their house at Christmas.
4 Banks charge customers to cancel a cheque.
5 People dip biscuits in their tea before eating them.
6 Most police officers don't carry guns.
7 People say "Bless you!" when someone sneezes.
8 Young children are vaccinated against a number of diseases.

2 Complete the texts below with one preposition in each gap.

The practice (1) .... planting trees to offset the impact (2) .... the environment (3) .... carbon emissions from flights has been criticized by environmental groups. They say that trees planted now will take many years to grow and their benefits will only be noticed (4) .... a very long period of time. The effects (5) .... pollution from aircraft are, however, immediate.

Floods are a regular occurrence on the Danube at this time (6) .... the year, but this spring, the river has reached record levels. Thousands of people in Bulgaria and Romania have had to be evacuated from areas affected (7) .... the floods. The impact (8) .... agriculture in the region has also been severe. Although floods have always been a natural part of life, many believe that the current levels of flooding are a consequence (9) .... human intervention. The practice (10) .... building on flood plains especially means that excess water has nowhere to go.

3 Match the two halves of the sentences.

1	There will be an inquiry into the behaviour	of the time.
2	People don't realise the health consequences	of the police at the march.
3	Tourists aren't familiar with the American custom	of heavy drinking.
4	The shop was shut down for the duration	of trade unions.
5	You should try to get out of the habit	of his resignation.
6	The report assesses the potential impact	of five to ten years.
7	We have seen the increasing political influence	of tipping 15% in restaurants.
8	He works away from home most	of adding salt to your food.
9	You pay the loan off gradually over a period	of the war.
10	Many were surprised by the timing	of climate change.

4 The paragraph below contains 10 errors. Edit the text by finding and correcting the errors.

The effects to employees of working for long hours can be very serious, especially over a scale of time. Businesses need to look at whether their working practises encourage overwork. We should consider the impact of long working times on health and for family life. Children whose parents are at work most of the times really miss out. Where parents have very little free-time to spend with their family, children often develop problems with their behaviours and get into bad habits. It is easy for children to get out of control because their busy parents leave very little influence on them.

5 Choose the best adjective from the box to complete the sentences. Use a good learner's dictionary to check any collocations you are not sure about.

common	annoying	unsocial	knock-on
serious	big	harmful	bad

1 Cuts to the service could have .... consequences for disabled people.

2 Nurses are often expected to work .... hours.

3 People claim the cartoon series is a .... influence on young people.

4 Always wear sun cream to avoid the .... effects of the sun.

5 The congestion charge has had a .... impact on traffic flow in the city.

6 It is .... practice to include a 10% service charge on the bill.

7 She has the .... habit of tapping her pen on the desk.

8 The rise in oil prices will have a .... effect on other industries.

28 Using nouns: *appearance* and *communication*

1 Tick the correct sentence in each pair.

1 a Public art can have a considerable effect on the outlook of public spaces.
  b Public art can have a considerable effect on the appearance of public spaces.
2 a We need better communications between parents and teachers.
  b We need better communication between parents and teachers.

The *appearance* of something is the way it looks and a person's *appearance* is the way they look (their face, body, hair, etc.) and the way they dress:
*Artificial ingredients are sometimes added to enhance the taste or **appearance of** food.*
*Many young women spend a lot of time on their **appearance**. (not ~~their appearances~~)*

A person's *looks* refers to how attractive they are – their face, etc. but not their clothes:
*She had gone grey and **lost her looks**. (= she was not as attractive as before)*

A person's *outlook* is the way they think about their life and the future:
*The accident completely changed **her outlook on life**. She enjoys each day at a time.*

Communication is an uncountable noun and refers to the act of talking to people:
*The job requires excellent **communication skills**.*
*Email is now our main **means of communication**. (not ~~mean of communication~~)*

Communications (plural) refers to all the methods of sending information, for example by telephone, email, post, etc.:
*They produce mobile phones and other **communications** equipment.*

2 Correct the mistake below.

I don't think you should judge people on their appearances.

INTERVIEW ROOM

I don't think ....

3 Underline the correct words.

1 In a digital age, face-to-face *communication/communications* is still important.
2 He's rather scruffy and doesn't pay much attention to his *appearance/looks*.
3 People spend more money on their health and *beauty/appearance* than in the past.
4 Good *communication/communications* are essential for a successful business.
5 He denied that he got the film contract just because of his *looks/appearances*.
6 She's very different from her sister in *outlook/look* and attitudes.
7 Don't be put off by the external *appearance/looks* of the building.
8 Mobiles are now a vital means of *communication/communications* in remote areas.

Using nouns and adjectives: *male* or *men*?

1 Tick the correct sentence in each pair.

1 a There are now more opportunities for females within the police service.

  b There are now more opportunities for women within the police service.

2 a The chart shows the number of hours worked by men and women employees.

  b The chart shows the number of hours worked by male and female employees.

Male and *female* can be used as nouns, but they are only used in very formal or technical writing, or when talking about animals rather than people:
*The **male tree frog** sings to attract a **female**.*

In most spoken and written contexts, we use the nouns *man/men* or *woman/women*:
*Nursing and teaching degrees still attract more **women** than **men**.*
*The life expectancy for an average **man** in Switzerland is 77 years.*

Male and *female* are used as adjectives in written and spoken English:
*We have a roughly equal number of **male** and **female students**.*
*All the **candidates** on the shortlist were **male**.*

In informal conversation, people sometimes use *woman* or *lady* before another noun instead of *female*. Some people do not like *lady* used in this way:
a woman/lady doctor   *a woman/lady golfer*   *a woman driver*
*She was the first **woman president** of Ireland.*

2 Correct the mistake below.

I think females can do all kinds of jobs.

I think ....

3 Complete the sentences using *male, female, man, men, woman* or *women*.

1 On average, women earn 30 percent less than their .... colleagues.

2 .... and .... managers bring different skills to their position.

3 The competition is open to both .... and ....

4 Women sometimes prefer to see a .... doctor.

5 She married a .... who was twenty years her senior.

6 The .... lays her eggs in a hole in the sand.

7 Mrs Thatcher was the first .... Prime Minister in the UK.

8 Children who do not live with their father do not have a strong .... role model.

Using nouns and adjectives: *Britain, British* or *Briton*?

1 Tick the correct sentence in each pair.

1 a The most popular country for Britons to visit in 1999 was France.
   b The most popular country for British to visit in 1999 was France.
2 a The company is based in the Thai capital, Bangkok.
   b The company is based in the Thailand capital, Bangkok.

To talk about things which belong to or come from a place, we use an adjective:
a French word   *Thai food*   *Most of the students are Asian.*
UK and *US* (not *USA*) are sometimes used as adjectives before a noun, especially
referring to a company, a system or an organisation:
the UK government   *UK companies*   *British food* (not usually ~~UK food~~)
the US legal system   *the US government* (not ~~the USA government~~)

The noun to refer to a person from a place is usually the same word as the adjective:
an American, an Australian, a German, a Thai, an Asian, a European
Some nationalities have a different word to refer to a person from that country:
an Englishman/Englishwoman, a Frenchman/Frenchwoman, a Dutchman/Dutchwoman
a Dane (Denmark), *a Filipino* (the Philippines), *a Finn* (Finland), *a New Zealander,*
a Pole (Poland), *a Spaniard* (Spain), *a Swede* (Sweden), *a Turk* (Turkey)
Briton is often used to refer to a person from Britain in writing and news reports, but
in conversation we usually talk about *a British person/man/woman.*
☆ There are some common informal words for nationalities, such as *Brit, Aussie* and
Kiwi. These are not appropriate in more formal writing.

2 Correct the mistake below.

Italy food is popular all over the world.

.... popular all over the world.

3 Complete the gaps using the best noun or adjective for the country given.

1 (*Germany*) This could have a serious effect on the .... economy.
2 (*Britain*) Several tourists were injured in the accident, including four ....
3 (*France*) According to statistics, ... contributed $5.4 million in aid.
4 (*Sweden*) The average .... drinks 7.8 kilograms of coffee a year.
5 (*China*) The population of .... is more than 1.3 billion.
6 (*Australia*) The scheme was set up by the .... government.
7 (*USA*) Machines selling fizzy drinks are to be banned in all .... schools.
8 (*Africa*) AIDS is the most common cause of death in many .... countries.

1 Complete the paragraph below with an appropriate noun or adjective in each space. Add any articles (*a/an/the*) where necessary.

What do we drink?

Bottled water		Carbonated soft drinks	
Country	**Amount***	**Country**	**Amount***
1 Italy	155 litres	1 United States	216 litres
2 France	146.6 litres	2 Ireland	126 litres
3 Belgium	117.1 litres	3 Canada	119.8 litres
4 Switzerland	111.2 litres	4 Norway	119.8 litres
5 Germany	109.2 litres	5 Belgium	102.9 litres
6 Austria	86.5 litres	6 Australia	100.1 litres
7 United States	46.8 litres	7 United Kingdom	96.5 litres
8 Canada	29.7 litres	8 Netherlands	96.1 litres
9 Ireland	27.1 litres	9 New Zealand	84.2 litres
10 United Kingdom	25.4 litres	10 Sweden	82.4 litres

*Litres per person per year

The tables show the amount of bottled water and carbonated soft drinks consumed per person per year in countries around the world. Bottled water is most popular in (**example**) ....Italy.......................... , with the average (1) .... drinking 155 litres per year. (2) .... ranks second with 146.6 litres per person. In fact, the top six countries in terms of consumption of bottled water are all (3)....................................... . (4) .... and (5) .... come next in seventh and eighth positions, with (6) .... and (7) .... consuming the least bottled water of the countries mentioned. (8) .... people only drink an average of 25.4 litres of bottled water a year.

The country which consumes by far the greatest quantity of soft drinks per capita is (9) .... (10) .... drink an average of 216 litres each a year, that's almost double the consumption of any other country. Another (11) .... country, (12) .... , comes third in the table, while (13) .... drinkers are ranked at number two, consuming an average of 126 litres annually. (14) .... drink approximately the same quantity of soft drinks as (15) ...., that is 119.8 litres per year, whereas another (16) .... country, (17) ...., only just features in the top ten, with the average (18) .... drinking 82.4 litres a year. The (19) .... and the (20) .... drink similar amounts, 96.5 and 96.1 litres per year respectively.

2 Complete the sentences using one of the words from the box in each gap. Use each word only once.

appearance	communication	communications	female
females	looks	outlook	women

1 There has been a breakdown in .... between the two sides in the dispute.
2 In 2005, 127 .... were elected to the British Parliament, just 19.7% of MPs.
3 A fresh coat of paint can make a huge difference to the .... of a building.
4 There needs to be better regulation of the .... industry in the UK.
5 There has been an increase in the proportion of .... politicians at a local level.
6 He obviously gets his good .... from his father.
7 The .... are smaller and have dark brown feathers.
8 I think travelling abroad has really broadened my ....

3 Vocabulary extension. Countries and nationalities crossword

Across →
1 The continent including Australia and New Zealand
4 From Poland
8 A person from the Philippines
9 The home of the Dutch
11 The continent including China and India
13 From Switzerland
17 A person from Denmark
19 The home of the Chinese
20 A person from Scotland
21 From the United States
22 A man from Ireland
23 The cold area at the far north of the world (3,6)

Down ↓
1 People from Austria
2 Another name for 9 across (3,11)
3 People from Iceland
4 From Pakistan
5 From Hungary
6 The home of the Nepalese
7 A person from Poland
10 The home of Laotians
12 A person from Spain
14 A man from Wales
15 From Scotland
16 From Israel
18 The ocean west of the Americas

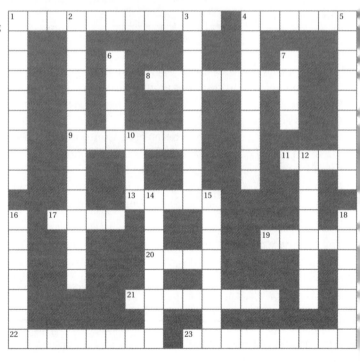

Answer key

Unit 1
1 1 b
   2 a
2 the importance of a balanced diet
3 1 bad for **the** heart
   2 *correct*
   3 benefit from **the** development of
   4 unhappy about **the** quality of
   5 *correct*
   6 *correct*
   7 depending on **the** standard of accommodation
   8 the role of **the** family

Unit 2
1 1 a
   2 b
2 have an equal chance of winning
3 1 Only a small number of troublemakers were responsible for the problems.
   2 Computers play a very important role in education nowadays.
   3 She can't afford to study on a full-time basis.
   4 Teenagers should be allowed a greater degree of freedom.
   5 They have a slightly different approach to studying.
   6 We had a one-week intensive training course.
   7 There has been a gradual increase in the number of thefts.
   8 They offer quite a wide variety of courses.

Unit 3
1 1 a
   2 a
2 Heathrow Airport on 12th January at 5.30 in the morning
3 1 Visitors to China should remember not to give a clock as a present.
   2 These customs are common in Muslim countries such as Saudi Arabia.
   3 She started work for Microsoft in July 2005.
   4 I went to university in Geneva in Switzerland.
   5 We took a taxi from York Station to the Royal York Hotel in the city centre.
   6 This is a photo of me on Wall Street when we visited New York last summer.
   7 The Red Cross works throughout the world and not just in Third World countries.
   8 She hopes to compete for France in the European Championships in August.

Test 1
1 1 the concentration; the stomach
   2 an incredibly long time
   3 – improvements; – quality; – efficiency
   4 A high percentage
   5 a significant number
   6 a sharp decline; the proportion of
   7 the extended family
   8 to a certain extent
   9 a basic education
   10 the recruitment of
   11 the significance of
   12 – excellent communication skills
2 14 December, 1950; throughout **the** **w**orld; in **the** resolution of; in **G**eneva, **S**witzerland; the **o**rganisation; safeguard **the** rights; **A** large proportion; in **the** **T**hird **W**orld; in **A**frica and **A**sia; in **E**urope and **the** **U**nited **S**tates
3 1 **O**dile is French. **S**he was born **in** Lyon **on** 21 September, 1968. **S**he moved **to** Britain 20 years ago and now has **B**ritish citizenship. **S**he speaks English fluently but she still has quite **a** strong French accent.

2 Corinne lives with her husband, **S**teve, near **M**elbourne, **A**ustralia. **S**teve is **A**ustralian but **C**orinne has **a G**erman mother and **an A**merican father. **S**he was born **in the U**nited **S**tates and met **S**teve while they were both working **in E**urope.

3 André is **a** travel photographer. **He** lives **in S**witzerland but he spends **a** large part of the year travelling around **the** world. **L**ast summer, he went on **a** long trip **to S**outh America to photograph ancient Inca temples.

4 1 The council wants to encourage the development of new businesses.

2 His main role is to assess the quality of service for/to customers.

3 There has been an increase in the transportation of goods by road.

4 Whether mothers return to work often depends on the availability of childcare.

5 Many of the changes are due to the growth of tourism in the region.

Unit 4

1 1 b
   2 b

2 whether I should call him or wait for him to call me

3 1 whether   5 if
   2 when   6 whether
   3 when   7 if
   4 whether   8 when

Unit 5

1 1 a
   2 b

2 Inevitably, there's always

3 1 if, for example, you forget …
   2 To sum up, I'd like …
   3 Statistics can, however, be misleading.
   4 countries, such as Bangladesh, are …
   5 Furthermore, not everyone …
   6 Contact sports, like rugby, will inevitably …
   7 *no changes needed*
   8 We will, of course, reimburse …

Unit 6

1 1 b
   2 a

2 dog's looking really bored. Where's its lead?

3 1 It's; someone's   5 don't
   2 can't   6 Let's
   3 that's   7 isn't
   4 government's   8 who's

Test 2

1 an energy crisis and, **undoubtedly,** one of the keys; It **isn't, however,** as straightforward; **Firstly,** we need …; We could look, **for example,** at ways; Many measures, **such as** roof insulation and double-glazing, are often; **Moreover,** many poor people; houses which **aren't** as easy; **Secondly, it's** much easier; **However,** for a developing country; **In conclusion,** we can say; some will, **inevitably,** need help.

2 1 if   5 whether
   2 who's   6 For example
   3 when   7 its
   4 if   8 whether

3 1 is, of course, slower
   2 people, especially single parents, these rises will cause
   3 are, however, alternatives to surgery
   4 people, such as those in flats, compost bins are
   5 are, therefore, a number of precautions we would
      or are a number of precautions, therefore, we would
      or are a number of precautions we would, therefore,
   6 are, to a certain extent, responsible for
      or are responsible, to a certain extent, for
   7 people, for instance, are more vulnerable to
   8 delays are, unfortunately,
      or delays, unfortunately, are

4
1 whether   5 its
2 obviously   6 when
3 It's   7 If
4 However   8 like

Unit 7

1 1 b
   2 a
2 more practice before you take your test
3 1 believe
   2 government; environmental
   3 hygiene
   4 *no errors*
   5 benefit; countries
   6 programmes
   7 proportion; achieve
   8 *no errors*

Unit 8

1 1 b
   2 b
2 talk face-to-face nowadays
3 1 … said they were satisfied, **whereas** only 60% of men …
   2 clean and **everything** was neatly…
   3 *no errors*
   4 … the health and **well-being** of all our residents.
   5 *no errors*
   6 … research into the **lifespan** of people living in the **countryside**.
   7 **Maybe** learning a foreign language …
   8 … runs **twenty-six** hostels spread **throughout** the country.

Unit 9

1 1 a
   2 b
2 that's a bit inappropriate/unsuitable for a job interview
3 1 30-year
   2 inexpensive
   3 well-educated
   4 single-storey
   5 hard-working
   6 well-balanced
   7 week-long
   8 unsuitable

Test 3

1 express my **dissatisfaction**; standard of **accommodation**; I **received**; booked a **non-smoking double room**; a rather **impolite** receptionist; it was a **fifth-floor** room; the lift was **out of order**. **Even though** I had a number of heavy bags, **nobody** offered; **Moreover**, when; the **incorrect** key; found **someone** to exchange; cramped and **ill-equipped**, with no phone; on your **website**.
2 1 time-saving devices
   2 well-equipped/fully-equipped kitchens
   3 a rather short-tempered man
   4 a 200-year-old castle
   5 a short-lived ceasefire
   6 a 5-year prison sentence
3 1 programmes
   2 lifestyle
   3 fully-trained
   4 twenty-five
   5 practise
   6 full-size
   7 12-month
   8 dependent
4 1 Good-looking, easy-going, 30-year-old man seeks well-educated young woman.
   2 Attractive, well-equipped, two-bedroom holiday cottage set in breath-taking countryside. Non-smokers only please.
   3 Treat yourself to a one-to-one consultation with one of our fully-qualified beauty therapists for professional advice on your make-up and hairstyle.
   4 Fed up with overcrowded, overpriced resorts? Why not try a weekend break in Sofia? Check our website for details of inexpensive, two-day breaks in Bulgaria's historic capital.

Unit 10

1 1 a
   2 b

2 on his website, he left the club for personal reasons

3 1 Young people copy (the) role models they see on television.

    2 The band (have) cancelled the/their performance for personal reasons.

    3 The building is/was closed to the public due to safety concerns.

    4 The Prime Minister appeared last night on a BBC current affairs programme.

    5 She didn't give a reason for being late.

    6 Many people now book (their) holidays on the internet.

    7 They spend eight hours a/per day working on a computer.

    8 Then an error message suddenly appeared on the/my screen.

Unit 11

1 1 a

    2 a

2 do you spend a month on hair products

3 1 … spend huge sums **on** advertising.

    2 … provide customers **with** better information …

    3 … a problem I think you can help me **with**.

    4 … to increase investment **in** education.

    5 … the provision **of** more special lanes for cyclists.

    6 … no facilities provided **for** passengers with …

    7 Spending **on** photographic film …

    8 … to help guests **with** their bags.

Unit 12

1 1 a

    2 b

2 a sudden surge in ice cream sales

3 1 in   5 in

    2 of   6 in

    3 in   7 of

    4 of   8 in

Test 4

1 1 of   9 on

    2 of   10 on

    3 in   11 on

    4 of   12 of

    5 in   13 for

    6 in   14 on

    7 in   15 on

    8 in   16 of

2 a dramatic increase **in** the number; look **on** the internet; deals **on** their websites; facilities **for** their passengers; a few euros **on** a flight; reduction **in** the cost; explosion **in** the number; growth **of/in** air travel; changes **in** patterns; investment **in** many regional airports

3 1 reduction of 25% / a 25% reduction in (the number of) injuries

    2 a great deal of variation in the availability of this treatment from one region to another.

    3 a rise of 40% / a 40% rise in house prices

    4 reach a peak of around 30°C in summer

    5 (to make) improvements in computer access for students

    6 more/greater investment in staff training

4 1 My main reason for giving up my car was environmental.

    2 Improvements in local public transport mean that I just don't need a car.

    3 I decided to get rid of my car for a number of different reasons.

    4 It wasn't economic to run a car any more due to the high cost of fuel.

    5 I found I was spending too much money on repairs.

Unit 13

1 1 b

    2 a

2 of dogs said they preferred Woofies

3 1 France has the greatest number **with** 12 million …

2 ... fluctuated between 3.5 **and** 4%.

3 ... 18,000 yen **at** the current exchange rate.

4 ... only available **for** the UK.

5 *correct*

6 *correct*

7 ... least popular destination **with** only 6% of flights.

8 12% **of** interviewees ...

Unit 14

1 1 b
  2 a

2 the proportion of an average day

3
1	percentage	5	proportion
2	unemployment	6	crime
3	diagram	7	percentage
4	percent	8	graph

Unit 15

1 1 b
  2 a

2 reaches a peak in July

3 1 rose
  2 see
  3 reached
  4 compares *or* shows
  5 illustrates *or* shows
  6 suggest *or* show
  7 dropped *or* fell
  8 reduce

Test 5

1
1	bar chart	8	in
2	compares	9	rate
3	for	10	fell
4	see	11	pie chart
5	with	12	percentage
6	drops	13	comes
7	graph	14	percent

2 1 ... between 2000 **and** 2005.
  2 ... teachers **at** all levels.
  3 ... rates of pay **for** workers ...
  4 ... only 5% **of** senior posts ...
  5 ... the survey **with** a 75% ...
  6 ... proportion **of** the overall budget ...
  7 ... rising **at** a rate of 1.8mm ...
  8 ... the data **for** London ...

9 Three-quarters **of** customers ...

10 ... rates **of** pay ...

3 1 The chart shows the percentage of employees who/that work late approximately three days per/a week.

2 The figures show the average number of days holiday for skilled and unskilled workers.

3 The rate of tooth decay dropped (by) ten percent between 1980 and 1990.

4 We can see that two-thirds of children watch more than four hours of television a/per day.

5 Zurich is/was/comes second in the table of the most expensive European cities.

6 The first graph compares the percentages of single-parent families in/for different income groups.

4 *Movement or trend upwards:* boost, jump, gain, soar, peak, surge, rocket
Movement or trend downwards: downturn, trough, halve, shrink, plummet, slump, diminish
Slow change: gradually, steady
Fast change: dramatically, sharp, steep, rapid

Unit 16

1 1 b
  2 a

2 in the number of butterflies this year

3 1 ... has **the** lowest **number of** people ...

2 ... about **the amount of** time ...

3 ... at **the number of** customers ...

4 ... compared **the amount of** leisure time ...

5 ... generate **a large amount of** money ...

6 ... show **the total number of** overseas students ...

7 ... measured **the average number of** times ...

8 ... do **the same amount of** work ...

Unit 17

1 1 b
      2 b
2 compared with/to my last dog
3 1 … **compared** to 64.6 million in 2006.
      2 *correct*
      3 In **comparison** with other writers …
      4 There is no comparison **between** watching …
      5 … **compared** to 62% …
      6 … by males **than** (by) females
      7 *correct*
      8 … when **compared** to Mauritius …

Unit 18

1 1 a
      2 a
2 in contrast/on the other hand, prefers less energetic hobbies
3 1 in contrast
      2 on the contrary
      3 in contrast to
      4 contrast between
      5 on the other hand / in contrast
      6 in contrast to
      7 in contrast / on the other hand
      8 on the other hand

Test 6

1 1 amount
      2 in contrast
      3 compares
      4 number
      5 in contrast to
      6 in comparison with
      7 amount
      8 compared to
2 1 The sample … boys and girls.
      2 They are expected … calls per hour.
      3 The job … travelling.
      4 There is only … space available.
      5 We try … damage to the environment.
      6 There are … players in each team.
3 1 … a relatively low crime rate in comparison with/to other European countries.
      2 … in contrast to 78 years in the UK, 79 in France and nearly 81 in Japan.
      3 … is no comparison between mountain biking and track cycling.
      4 … made/drawn a comparison between them and the Beatles.
      5 … In the USA, on the other hand, students work their way through college.
4 in comparison **with/to** other EU countries; income in tax **compared** with only 29.7%; almost half **that of** workers in Germany; **In contrast**, Scotland; Compared **with/to** those living in other regions; the highest **proportion/percentage** of people from non-white ethnic groups; 29 percent of its population, **compared** with 8 percent
5 1 fair   6 direct
      2 increasing   7 large
      3 marked   8 enormous
      4 limited   9 stark
      5 same   10 certain

Unit 19

1 1 a
      2 b
2 were meant to come in evening dress
3 1 clothing   5 times
      2 countries   6 equipment
      3 experience   7 advertising
      4 software   8 transport

Unit 20

1 1 a
      2 a
2 love playing with the animals
3 1 allows   5 receives
      2 eat, need   6 are
      3 mean   7 varies
      4 is   8 have

Unit 21

1 1 b
      2 a
2 share them with your sister

3
1	them	5	it
2	it	6	they
3	it	7	them
4	them	8	their

Test 7

1
1	behaviour	6	shopping
2	information	7	help
3	damage	8	training
4	ideas	9	times
5	equipment	10	countries

2 **Research has** shown; young children **find** it easier; learning new languages **is** more difficult; but **it is** certainly not impossible; and **become** fluent speakers; the best **teaching** methods

In many western **countries**, obesity among children **is** increasing; overweight children **has** doubled; Some people **believe** that children **are** getting fatter; eating too much fast **food**; argue that **they are** not getting enough exercise.

New technology **allows** us; other **information** online; newspapers **are** necessary; or whether **they** will soon disappear; news websites which **are** updated; newspapers still **continue** to be printed and people **continue** to buy **them**.

3
1 … the main tourist attractions **are** least crowded
2 … your country **has** a hot climate – *verb form correct*
3 **Is** the weather hot …
4 What sort of dress **is** appropriate …
5 … women **cover** their heads – *verb form correct*
6 … women cover their heads and **wear** clothing …
7 … clothing which **covers** their arms and legs
8 … Egyptian cooking **uses** a lot of spices
9 … many dishes **contain** meat
10 … any websites which **have** information

4 C: computer, hour, aspect, nation, job
U: advice, accommodation, potential, heating, paperwork

Unit 22

1
1 b
2 a

2 to having a place of my own

3
1	are	5	was having
2	being	6	has *or* had
3	have *or* had	7	being
4	being	8	having

Unit 23

1
1 b
2 a

2 to attend daily training sessions

3
1	attend	5	join
2	provide	6	provides
3	attend	7	went to
4	given	8	give

Unit 24

1
1 a
2 a

2 give me one reason why I should give it back

3
1	give	5	have
2	deal with	6	have
3	make	7	make
4	committed	8	had

Test 8

1
1	joined	7	have
2	make	8	'm
3	give	9	given
4	being	10	go to
5	being	11	have
6	was having	12	being

2
1 I usually grab a sandwich at lunchtime rather than have a cooked meal.
2 Don't take a/the room without having a look first.
3 The building has/buildings have smoke alarms in every room.
4 He didn't give a/any reason for being late.

5 She is/She's quite shy and she doesn't really like being in the spotlight.

6 The young mums enjoy having a chat while the/their children play/are playing.

7 The villagers don't have access to clean water or health care.

8 There are advantages to being part of an organised tour group.

3 Nurses **attending** their annual conference; Health Service to **provide** better support; nurses from abroad **are** highly trained; UK hospitals **have** different working practices; they are not used to **having** the same responsibilities; many foreign nurses are not **provided with/given** proper training; not equipped to **deal with** the problems; without **being** rude; from colleagues **made** a big difference and **made** it easier to fit in.

4
1	made	6	make
2	have	7	gave
3	have	8	have
4	make	9	made
5	gives	10	give

Unit 25

1 1 b
  2 a

2 a British custom for a man to carry his new wife into their new home

3
1	customs	5	habits
2	practice	6	practice
3	habits	7	customs
4	custom	8	behaviour

Unit 26

1 1 b
  2 a

2 the effects of transport policy on wildlife

3 1 … have an effect **on** the health …
  2 … harmful **effect** on fish.
  3 … the **influence** of religion …
  4 *correct*
  5 … the **effects** of violent films.
  6 … the influence they **have** on …

7 … a devastating **effect** on …
8 *correct*

Unit 27

1 1 b
  2 b

2 the museum opening hours

3
1	time	5	timing
2	period	6	time
3	duration	7	period
4	hours	8	hours

Test 9

1
1	C	5	H
2	H	6	P
3	C	7	C
4	P	8	P

2
1	of	6	of
2	on	7	by
3	of	8	on
4	over	9	of
5	of	10	of

3 1 There will be … of the police at the march.
  2 People don't … of heavy drinking.
  3 Tourists aren't … of tipping 15% in restaurants.
  4 The shop … of the war.
  5 You should … of adding salt to your food.
  6 The report … of climate change.
  7 We have … of trade unions.
  8 He works … of the time.
  9 You pay … of five to ten years.
  10 Many were … of his resignation.

4 The effects **on** employees; working ~~for~~ long hours can; over a **period** of time; working **practices** encourage; long working **hours** on health and **on** family life; most of the **time** really; little **free time** to spend; problems with their **behaviour** and get into bad habits; parents **have** very little influence

5
1	serious	5	big
2	unsocial	6	common
3	bad	7	annoying
4	harmful	8	knock-on

Unit 28

1 1 b
   2 b

2 you should judge people on their appearance

3 1 communication
   2 appearance
   3 appearance
   4 communications
   5 looks
   6 outlook
   7 appearance
   8 communication

Unit 29

1 1 b
   2 b

2 women can do all kinds of jobs

3 1 male
   2 Male, female
   3 men, women
   4 female/woman/(lady)
   5 man
   6 female
   7 female/woman
   8 male

Unit 30

1 1 a
   2 a

2 Italian food is

3 1 German
   2 Britons (British people)
   3 France
   4 Swede
   5 China
   6 Australian
   7 American/US
   8 African

Test 10

1 1 Italian
   2 France
   3 European
   4 The United States (The US)
   5 Canada
   6 Ireland
   7 the United Kingdom (the UK)
   8 British
   9 the United States (the US)
   10 Americans
   11 North American
   12 Canada
   13 Irish
   14 Norwegians
   15 Canadians
   16 Scandinavian
   17 Sweden
   18 Swede
   19 British
   20 Dutch

2 1 communication
   2 women
   3 appearance
   4 communications
   5 female
   6 looks
   7 females
   8 outlook

3 Across
   1 Australasia
   4 Polish
   8 Filipino
   9 Holland
   11 Asia
   13 Swiss
   17 Dane
   19 China
   20 Scot
   21 American
   22 Irishman
   23 The Arctic

Down
   1 Austrians
   2 The Netherlands
   3 Icelanders
   4 Pakistani
   5 Hungarian
   6 Nepal
   7 Pole
   10 Laos
   12 Spaniard
   14 Welshman
   15 Scottish
   16 Israeli
   18 Pacific

Acknowledgements

The author would like to thank her colleagues and students at Bristol University Language Centre for bringing many of these mistakes to life.

The author and publishers are grateful to the following for permission to reproduce copyright material. While every effort has been made, it has not always been possible to identify the sources of all the material used, or to trace the copyright holders. If any omissions are brought to our notice, we will be happy to include the appropriate acknowledgements on reprinting.

For the logo UNHCR on p.8: used by kind permission of the UN High Commissioner for Refugees; for the texts on p.23: 'Birth rates continue to rise' and 'Spending on books dwarfed by ICT', used by permission of bbc.co.uk; for the text on p.53: 'What do we drink?', statistics used by permission of NationMaster.com.

Illustrated by Julian Mosedale

The Cambridge Learner Corpus
This book is based on information from the Cambridge Learner Corpus, a collection of over 90,000 exam papers from Cambridge ESOL. It shows real mistakes students make, and highlights which parts of English cause particular problems for learners.

The Cambridge Learner Corpus has been developed jointly with the University of Cambridge ESOL Examinations and forms part of the Cambridge International Corpus.

To find out more, visit
www.cambridge.org/elt/corpus